El Alamein 1942

COMBAT

Eighth Army Soldier

VERSUS

Italian Soldier

David Greentree

Illustrated by Adam Hook

OSPREY PUBLISHING
Bloomsbury Publishing Plc
Kemp House, Chawley Park, Cumnor Hill, Oxford OX2 9PH, UK
29 Earlsfort Terrace, Dublin 2, Ireland
1385 Broadway, 5th Floor, New York, NY 10018, USA
E-mail: info@ospreypublishing.com
www.ospreypublishing.com

OSPREY is a trademark of Osprey Publishing Ltd

First published in Great Britain in 2024

A catalogue record for this book is available from the British Library.

ISBN: PB 9781472863416; eBook 9781472863386;
ePDF 9781472863393; XML 9781472863409

24 25 26 27 28   10 9 8 7 6 5 4 3 2 1

Maps by www.bounford.com
Index by Rob Munro
Typeset by PDQ Digital Media Solutions, Bungay, UK
Printed and bound in India by Repro India Ltd.

Osprey Publishing supports the Woodland Trust, the UK's leading
woodland conservation charity.

To find out more about our authors and books visit
www.ospreypublishing.com. Here you will find extracts, author
interviews, details of forthcoming events and the option to sign up for
our newsletter.

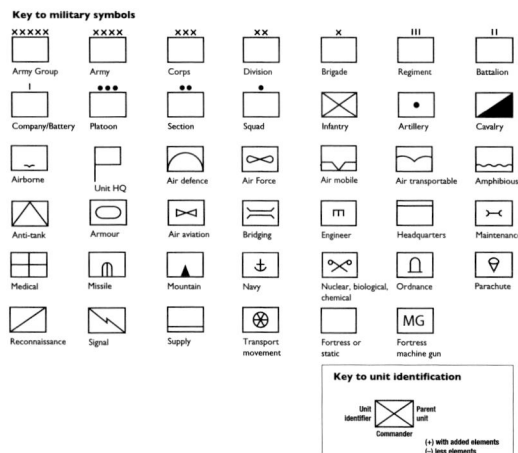

CONTENTS

Introduction

During World War II's Desert War (1940–43), armour was seen as the decisive weapon because terrain did not limit its mobility. Rock-hard or sandy surfaces made entrenchments difficult to build. Infantry needed landmines to construct effective defensive positions. The lack of natural barriers meant open flanks abounded, which in turn meant enveloping the enemy was nearly always possible. Lines were often not contiguous because there were not enough men to cover the length of the front line. Supplies had to be sent by sea, disembarked at the limited number of ports, and then transported by motor vehicles to the front. If the front was closer to the port of disembarkation the army could quickly rebuild after a defeat; if further away the army with the initiative could find itself soon running out of steam, particularly if enemy supplies could not be utilized. This explained the movement of the front line, with decisive results proving to be difficult to attain.

The small, highly mobile Western Desert Force's defeat of a static and immobile Italian army during December 1940–February 1941 suggested

to the British that they only had to place tanks on an enemy's lines of communication to win a campaign. British generals thought that infantry did not need to cooperate closely with tanks and enemy tanks did not need to be targeted offensively by anti-tank guns. Rather, tanks could disperse to harass the enemy and demoralize him. Artillery would be dispersed to support these mobile columns. This approach would only work, however, against an enemy lacking motor transport.

When Generalleutnant Erwin Rommel and the Deutsches Afrikakorps deployed to North Africa during March 1941 the British were rudely awakened. With British infantry units not possessing armour support, the danger was that they would suffer crippling losses.

German armour soon isolated the weakened Allied force garrisoning the crucial port of Tobruk, Libya, and drove the Allied field units back to the Libya–Egypt border. Allied infantry were able to hold on to the port, however, prompting a successful Allied relief attempt during late 1941, known as Operation *Crusader*. With the Allied defenders once again weakened because of the need to send men and *matériel* to the Pacific to counter the threat from Japan, Rommel was reinforced and, with supplies from Europe having reached North Africa safely, launched another offensive, taking him to the Gazala Line by March 1942.

Seeking to guard against enemy armour more effectively, during May 1942 the British forces holding the Gazala Line employed a static defence based on brigade boxes, with supporting artillery units issued piecemeal. By enveloping the forward line of Allied boxes, Rommel placed his armour on the boxes' supply lines and thereby prompted Eighth Army to attack with its armour, suffering huge losses in the process but substantially depleting the German armour. The British tanks had no infantry to take on the Axis anti-tank gun line, deployed by Rommel on the eastern side of the 'Cauldron', the term used to describe his surrounded position, and Allied counter-attacks failed. Italian formations had the time to get through British minefields to establish supply lines to Rommel. British generals now understood that the tank alone could not win battles: close cooperation between tanks, infantry and artillery was required. The decentralized theory of command based on the brigade as the main combined-arms unit did not succeed at Gazala because Allied firepower was dispersed, with 25-pdr field guns sent to brigades facing enemy tanks rather than infantry or gun positions because the 2-pdr anti-tank gun was ineffective. Only when the Allied forces deployed the 6-pdr anti-tank gun during the summer of 1942 did this change. The cost was high: Tobruk fell to the Axis forces on 20 June and Rommel pursued the demoralized Eighth Army through the Egyptian town of Mersa Matruh and back to El Alamein, close to the Nile Delta.

During the 1930s, the Italian government spent heavily on its military, but Italian participation in the Second Italo-Ethiopian War (1935–37) and the Spanish Civil War (1936–39) limited spending on infrastructure. Money was wasted because of financial corruption, and incompetence by administrators. The fascist principle of national self-sufficiency was expensive and imported raw materials had a high price. Benito Mussolini and his generals knew Italy was not ready for war in 1940; they wanted to wait until 1943. In June 1940, however, Mussolini thought taking advantage of France's looming defeat would be an easy proposition; imperial dreams would be realized quickly. His decision to invade Greece in October 1940 proved to be a huge mistake, the campaign costing the Italian forces 39,000 killed and 51,000 wounded. The Italian soldier paid the price of Mussolini's miscalculations, though many supported their leader's imperial ambitions; fascist propaganda had fed them fanciful ideas of Italian nationalism. Others would fight with stoic resignation.

This group of Indian Army soldiers at Cairo railway station on 12 November 1942 includes a number of Gurkhas. One man, likely an officer as he is armed with a revolver, wears the 'Bombay bloomers' issued in the early part of the war. Prime Minister Churchill, among others in the British hierarchy, worried about the reliability of Indian soldiers. The British authorities believed that some elements of Indian society were committed to the fight, but other groups not as much. Men from the Punjab were seen as the martial class; men from Bengal by contrast were believed to exhibit anti-British tendencies. (Associated Press/Alamy Stock Photo)

The decision to invade Greece was taken when the Italian Army was in the process of implementing a partial demobilization; this was not halted and the ranks were instead filled with men with little or no training. Trained reservist officers and NCOs had returned to civilian life to be replaced by newer recruits. The Greek campaign ended with Italian defeat by April 1941. The Germans had to bail out the Italians by invading. The Italians then decided to recall demobilized reservists. The armour of the 'Ariete' Armoured Division and the motorized infantry belonging to the 101ᵃ Divisione motorizzata 'Trento' were not deployed to North Africa during late 1940 because Mussolini kept them in Italy to invade Yugoslavia. In the event, the German forces did not need them in Yugoslavia and they were shipped to North Africa from February 1941. The incompetent Italian commander in North Africa during Operation *Compass*, Generale d'armata Italo Gariboldi, was sacked and Generale d'armata Ettore Bastico, who had gained armour experience during the Spanish Civil War, took his place. Bastico had trained the armour; now he would reform the infantry.

During the spring of 1941 Mussolini told Bastico to expect another three armoured, five motorized and six infantry divisions with which he was to invade Egypt. Mussolini failed to understand that Italy could either build large, ineffective ground forces or a capable army of limited size. Italy simply did not possess the industrial capacity to equip the number of units he wanted to send; nor was the port capacity in Libya capable of handling the amount of traffic. Mussolini was then distracted by Operation *Barbarossa*, the Axis invasion of the Soviet Union launched on 22 June. He committed a semi-motorized force of 62,000 men and 5,500 motor vehicles to the operation. At the time, during the summer of 1941, only 6,500 Italian trucks were operational in North Africa. Knowing a larger Italian mechanized force would be sent to the Soviet Union in 1942, Generale d'armata Ugo Cavallero, the chief of Italy's general staff, wanted Rommel to launch only local counter-attacks in January 1942. Cavallero wanted the Italian Army to stay on the defence during 1942. The priority was the Eastern Front.

Destined for the Soviet Union, the 8ᵃ Armata was composed of 229,000 men, 22,300 motor vehicles and 1,100 guns. The modern guns Italy possessed would be sent, including the 210mm and most of the 149mm pieces; the newer 75mm guns would also go. This was all at the expense of the Italian forces in North Africa. The strategy agreed for North Africa involved a local offensive to take the Axis forces to the Egyptian border and the seizure of Malta by airborne forces. Rommel's successes in early June were in part due to the support of the Italian Army, ensuring the Gazala minefields could be breached. The success of the operation persuaded the Germans and Italians to cancel the Malta operation and go for the Nile Delta during July 1942.

The German summer offensive in the Soviet Union focused British Prime Minister Winston Churchill's attention on the Axis threat to the Middle Eastern oilfields. He thought defences in Iran and

An Italian infantry patrol with a Brixia mod. 35 light mortar during Operation *Crusader*, December 1941. A total of 150 infantry, armour and cavalry regiments formed 75 divisions in the Italian Army when Mussolini declared war on 10 June 1940. (DE AGOSTINI PICTURE LIBRARY/Getty Images)

Syria needed to be built by Allied formations transferred from the desert; but only if Rommel was driven back could these forces be transferred. The British command was encouraged to attempt an offensive. This was not a correct strategic appreciation, though, because the Germans, if successful, would not be in position to threaten Iran until early 1943. Rather than expending time on a potentially costly offensive, Eighth Army could have spent the time reorganizing. Instead, hasty assaults conducted throughout July and implemented with no prior practice, poor staff work and no common doctrine saw infantry break into Axis positions but Allied tanks fail to consolidate the gains made. Allied higher formations failed to work together and no cooperation or mutual understanding was evident.

The importance of infantry to the desert battlefield was revealed during the First and Second battles of El Alamein (1–27 July and 23 October–11 November 1942) when the British had closed flanks, protected by the Qattara Depression to the south and the Mediterranean Sea to the north. Infantry was not as exposed. Rommel had limited options to fight a mobile battle. He had to rely on his infantry to hold the line, with the Italians making up the majority of the Axis force. Out of 96,000 men at First El Alamein, 56,000 were Italian.

Commonwealth forces had always dominated the British infantry contingent; during late 1940, the Western Desert Force had 4th Indian Division as its infantry component. By July 1942, 80,000 of Eighth Army's 150,000 men were from Commonwealth formations. India sent the largest force; Australia deployed three divisions, though by July 1942 only 9th Australian Division belonged to Eighth Army; South Africa had two infantry divisions, though its commanders sought to limit casualties to these formations as political support for the war was wavering; and New Zealand deployed one division.

This study looks at the Australian, Indian and New Zealand infantry's contribution by focusing on the experiences of a specific battalion of each contingent during a battle against infantry belonging to Italian divisions during the two battles of El Alamein. On 15–16 July, the Indians with New Zealand support would fight the 17^a Divisione fanteria 'Pavia' for control of Ruweisat Ridge, situated near the middle of the British line and dominating the surrounding terrain. Then on 17 July the Australians would attack Makh Khad Ridge closer to the coast and fight motorized infantry belonging to the 101^a Divisione motorizzata 'Trieste'. Both operations would be limited successes; the same could not be said of the New Zealand attack on 'Trento' positions on 24 October. By then the infantry battle was key to the British plan.

The Italian formations would be constrained by their binary divisional structure. In 1934, Generale d'armata Federico Baistrocchi, the Italian Army's chief-of-staff, wanted a smaller army based on 25 powerful, well-armed and well-trained divisions, plus seven Blackshirt (voluntary militia for national

Emplaced Italian troops during Operation *Crusader*, November 1941. Note the depth of the entrenchment, not always possible with hard rock, suggesting the Italians spent some time in this location. A Breda 30 LMG can be seen, alongside a soldier using a Carcano M1891 cavalry carbine. The ammunition box with Breda clips is being carried backpack style by the soldier on the right. (DE AGOSTINI PICTURE LIBRARY/Getty Images)

MAP KEY

1 2 July: Having destroyed 18 Indian Brigade at Deir el Shein on 1 July, Generalfeldmarschall Rommel attempts to storm the El Alamein box, but fails because of massed Allied guns in the box.

2 5 July: 9th Australian Division deploys to Egypt and occupies the El Alamein box.

3 8–16 July: On 8 July, 26 Australian Brigade assaults Tel el Eisa, defeating elements of the 'Sabratha' Infantry Division. A joint German/Italian counter-attack takes back the height on 12 July. On 16 July, the Australians try to seize the height again; though this attempt fails, 'Sabratha' is nearly destroyed.

4 15 July: In the early morning, 5 Indian Brigade and 4 and 5 NZ brigades assault the 'Pavia' and 'Brescia' Infantry divisions on Ruweisat Ridge. Supported during the afternoon by 2 Armoured Brigade, the Indians succeed in taking and holding Point 64. Unsupported by 2 and 22 Armoured brigades, the New Zealanders fail to hold Point 63 at the western end of the ridge when attacked by German forces.

5 17 July: During the early morning, 24 Australian Brigade deploys 2/32 Battalion supported by 9th Divisional Cavalry against the II/65° Reggimento fanteria motorizzato on Makh Khad Ridge. In the darkness, A Coy overshoots the objective; the company is cut off and most surrender. During daylight, 2/43 Battalion passes through Makh Khad along the Qattara Track and with armour support heads towards positions of the 62° Reggimento fanteria motorizzato on Miteiriya Ridge. Though 2/43 Battalion reaches the initial heights, an Axis counter-attack forces the Australians to withdraw by the early afternoon.

6 22 July: Supported by 50 RTR, 2/32 Battalion again targets Makh Khad Ridge and Miteiriya Ridge. The III/61°

and III/62° Reggimenti fanteria motorizzato mostly hold their positions; lacking infantry support, British tanks reach the ridge but soon withdraw.

7 30 August–5 September: The battle of Alam el Halfa sees Rommel attempt to send his armour on a route south of Ruweisat Ridge and then north-east to Alam el Halfa Ridge. Italian infantry participation is limited, though the 'Trieste' Motorized Division does accompany the Italian tank force. Lieutenant-General Montgomery stations his armour west of the ridge directly supporting the infantry on the ridge's western end and defeats the Axis assault.

8 24 October: Operation *Lightfoot*, an Allied infantry assault by four infantry divisions designed to make channels through the dense minefields begins with infantry of 2nd NZ Division assaulting 5,000yd of front on Miteiriya Ridge. The II/62° Reggimento fanteria motorizzato, supported by elements of II./IR 382, defends the western end of the ridge against 21 NZ Battalion (5 NZ Brigade); the New Zealanders take the ridge but the battalion suffers 128 casualties.

9 27 October: 9th Australian Division continues infantry 'crumbling' operations further north, forcing Rommel to commit the 90. leichte Afrika-Division.

10 4 November: Following the success of Operation *Supercharge*, 51st (Highland) Division's infantry assault on the Rahman Track on 2 November, Montgomery launches 2nd NZ Division supported by 4 Light Armoured Brigade towards Fuka to pursue Rommel's withdrawing forces. Most Italian formations, especially the infantry, surrender because they lack motorized transport. 'Trieste' elements do escape, however.

security) divisions. With war with France and Britain looming, Generale d'armata Alberto Pariani, Baistrocchi's successor, implemented changes to make the Italian Army bigger; composed of 80 divisions in peacetime, it was to be expanded to 126 in wartime. In 1938 the binary division was created to make these changes possible, whereby this formation had only two infantry regiments. Mussolini could boast a larger army though the number of infantry regiments had not increased. On 10 June 1940, Mussolini had only 59 infantry, three Blackshirt, five mountain, three mobile, two motorized and three armoured divisions, excluding colonial formations or frontier guard units. The new structure hampered the Italian divisional commanders, however. Traditionally, the third infantry regiment was held in reserve. Now, to keep an infantry regiment in reserve only a single infantry regiment could be deployed in the first line. The artillery regiment was also downsized from four to three groups. During 1941–42, seven binary divisions fought in North Africa.

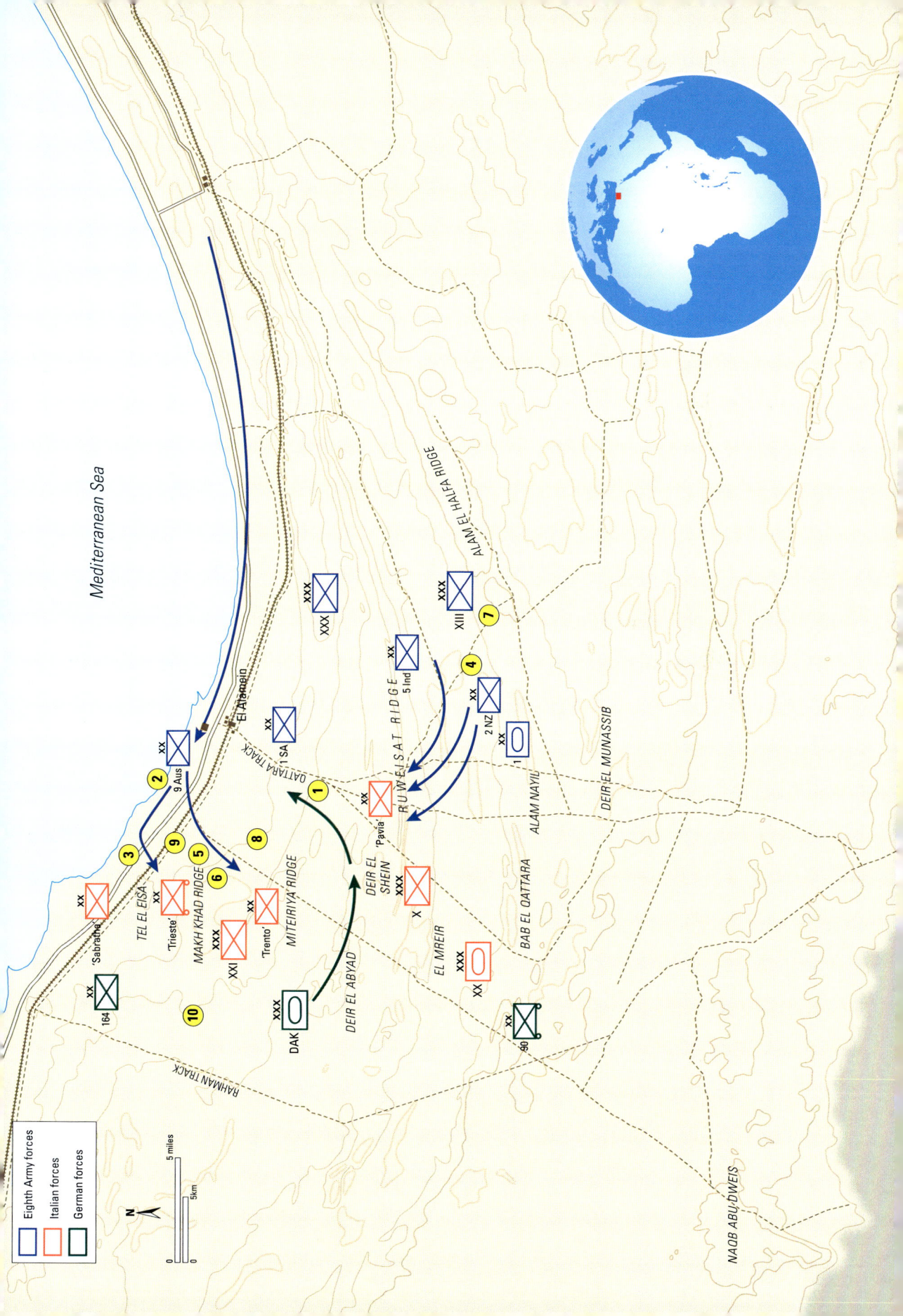

Mediterranean Sea

ALAM EL HALFA RIDGE

RUWEISAT RIDGE

XXX

XXX

XXX
XIII

7

XX
5 Ind

4

XX
2 NZ

XX
1 SA

XX
1

XX
Pavia

DEIR EL SHEIN

X

XXX

DEIR EL MUNASSIB

ALAM NAYIL

BAB EL QATTARA

EL MREIR

QATTARA TRACK

El Alamein

XX
9 Aus

2

1

XX
90

3

9

5

6

8

MITEIRIYA RIDGE

DEIR EL ABYAD

XX
164

10

XX
'Sabratha'

TEL EL EISA

XX
'Trieste'

MAKH KHAD RIDGE

XX
XXI
'Trento'

RAHMAN TRACK

XXX
DAK

NAQB ABU DWEIS

Eighth Army forces

Italian forces

German forces

N

5 miles

5km

The Opposing Sides

ORIGINS AND DOCTRINE

Commonwealth

Organization and doctrine were based on British practice. Each infantry division had three infantry brigades, each brigade three infantry battalions. The infantry organization mandated a lorry for each infantry platoon to haul equipment and the divisional motor pool was to possess enough motor transport to move a brigade. While motor transportation was good, infantry battalions lacked firepower because the support companies belonging to the battalion were re-formed as infantry companies. They needed field-gun support instead. The artillery of an infantry division included 72 25-pdr field guns; battery size was large, though, and requests for fire support from infantry battalions competed with each other. British practice through to mid-1942 was to decentralize the guns so each brigade possessed its own artillery component. British infantry tank formations would be attached to Commonwealth infantry to break through enemy defences when needed. Throughout most of the Desert War, however, the armour had small-calibre guns and few tanks capable of firing high-explosive ammunition.

After July 1942 the practice of decentralizing the guns to brigade groups persisted, but the New Zealanders and Australians did not obey this instruction. A policy of establishing mixed divisions with one armoured brigade and two infantry brigades was also under consideration. The Royal Armoured Corps (RAC) was keen, but the British cavalry regiments were not. The new scheme did not gain plaudits. The use of a chequerboard pattern of strongpoints on prominent features with armour roving between them was not accepted by Lieutenant-General B.G. Horrocks, GOC XIII Corps from August. He chose to place his armour on the most prominent features.

Troops of 4/11 Sikhs conduct a training exercise in Egypt, 6 August 1941. One man has a Bren gun while two crew a 2in mortar, a platoon-level support weapon. The .303 Bren LMG's rate of fire was theoretically approximately 500rd/min, though 120rd/min was practical. Using a bipod and fired from the prone position, effective range was about 600yd. (William Vanderson No 1 British Army Film & Photographic Unit/ FPG/Archive Photos/Getty Images)

Lieutenant-General B.L. Montgomery, from 13 August the new GOC Eighth Army, revived the concept of a division fighting as one, massing its guns as necessary and not dissipating them. By October 1942, Montgomery had amassed sufficient forces to break the Axis defences. He would attempt to 'crumble' the Axis infantry positions to force Rommel to counter-attack with armour on ground of Montgomery's choosing. Second El Alamein would initially be an infantry battle with field artillery and anti-tank guns shielding Montgomery's infantry from enemy tanks. With Rommel's armour weakened, Montgomery would use his armour to defeat the last Axis gun line and pursue the enemy.

By 1939, the Indian Army included 96 infantry battalions and numbered 43,500 British and 131,000 Indian soldiers. The North West Frontier needed to be permanently manned with three divisions; another four divisions of the field army had to be kept ready to defend against invasion from Afghanistan. Internal security was another concern, with 43 battalions tasked to assist the civil authorities to maintain law and order. In 1935, with war looming, India's commitment to Imperial defence was established at five brigades; two of them would go to Egypt. The outbreak of war led to the Army quickly expanding. By the end of 1940, 20,000 soldiers joined each month; by the end of 1941, the figure was 50,000 per month. At the end of 1941 the Army was composed of 900,000 men, 300,000 of whom were fighting abroad. By the end of 1942 it consisted of 1.8 million soldiers.

By the end of 1939, 4th Indian Division was sent to the Middle East, with British 16 Brigade attached to give the formation a third brigade. During

COMBAT

1

2

3

This corporal, a section leader, is armed with an M1928A1 Thompson submachine gun, a weapon widely carried by platoon and section commanders. His battalion will soon be targeted by Italian artillery and machine guns firing from concealed positions amid the scrub.

Weapons, dress and equipment

The corporal's M1928A1 Thompson submachine gun (**1**) is fitted with a 20-round magazine. Weighing 14lb loaded, the .45 Thompson was lethal at close range; the cyclic rate of fire was 675rd/min.

His khaki drill tropical shirt (**2**) has corporal's rank insignia on both upper arms. Ammunition pouches on his Pattern 1937 webbing (**3**) could hold either Bren-gun magazines or Thompson magazines. He wears long socks with puttees (**4**). He has a water bottle (**5**) and small pack (**6**) attached to his webbing.

Operation *Compass* the division represented nearly the entire infantry force of the Western Desert Force. Its men had plenty of time to train prior to the operation, but could not pursue the defeated Italians to Tripoli because they were sent to Eritrea. Alongside 5th Indian Division, during January–March 1941 4th Indian Division threw the Italians out of Ethiopia. The Ethiopian campaign cost the division 371 dead, 2,747 wounded and 155 missing. Subsequently deployed to Egypt, the division participated in Operation *Battleaxe*, the attempt to lift the siege of Tobruk during June 1941.

The Australian Army had a peacetime strength of 4,000 regular soldiers with a militia of 80,000 men. In 1939, the Australian government sent a volunteer force, known as the 2nd Australian Imperial Force (2nd AIF), to serve overseas and conscripted militia for home defence. Four divisions (6th, 7th, 8th and 9th) would be deployed overseas. Formed in Britain, 9th Australian Division was initially composed of 18 and 25 Australian brigades, but when 7th Australian Division was sent to Greece during March 1941, these brigades were exchanged for 20 and 26 Australian brigades belonging to 7th Australian Division as 18 and 25 Australian brigades were deemed to be better units. Originally part of 8th Australian Division, 24 Australian Brigade also served in 9th Australian Division. Formed on 1 July 1940, 24 Australian Brigade was initially composed of 2/25, 2/28 and 2/43 battalions; 2/25 Battalion was exchanged for 2/32 Battalion of 25 Australian Brigade because this brigade was destined to go to Greece during early 1941, and 2/32 Battalion had formed from surplus soldiers sent to Britain and was therefore less experienced.

During February 1941 the battalions of 24 Australian Brigade coalesced at Tobruk with Brigadier A.H.L. Godfrey assuming command. While 6th and 7th Australian divisions were sent to Greece, 9th Australian Division stayed in North Africa. Deployed to Benghazi, Libya, 20 and 26 Australian brigades withdrew to Tobruk when Rommel struck in March 1941. Until October 1941, when it was replaced by the British 70th Division, the defence of Tobruk cost 9th Australian Division 650 killed, 1,597 wounded and 917 taken prisoner. While 6th and 7th Australian divisions deployed to the Pacific in February 1942, 9th Australian Division remained in the Middle East.

After World War I, New Zealand maintained a division-sized formation until the 1930 Defence Act made military service voluntary. The Army was a small permanent force running a territorial force of brigade strength, capable of being expanded into a division during wartime. By 1939, regular personnel consisted of 76 officers and 134 other ranks. The Territorial Army (TA) had 778 officers and 9,586 other ranks active, but only 4,731 were infantry. When war began, the New Zealand government decided to keep the TA for home defence and raise a separate force for overseas service, organized into 2nd New Zealand Expeditionary Force (NZEF), composed of 4, 5 and 6 NZ brigades. Three successive echelons, each of three battalions, were trained, with the first (18, 19 and 20 NZ battalions) entering camp on 3 October 1939 and shipping out in December 1940, the next (21, 22 and 23 NZ battalions) entering camp on 12 January 1940 and sailing in May and the third (24, 25 and 26 NZ battalions) entering camp on 16 May 1940 and sailing by August 1940. The destination was Egypt. A machine-gun battalion (27 NZ Machine Gun Battalion), pioneer battalion (28 Māori Battalion), divisional cavalry

regiment, three artillery regiments (4, 5 and 6), one anti-tank regiment and three engineer companies accompanied the battalions. Major-General B.C. Freyberg, GOC 2nd NZ Division, wanted a tank battalion to form the basis for a brigade of armour to be part of his division, also including 27 NZ Machine Gun Battalion, another infantry battalion and the armoured cars of the cavalry. His request was vetoed because the organization specified by the British – two tank battalions, two infantry battalions and the armoured cars – could not be established by early 1941. Freyberg was thus keen on armour supporting his infantry during Operation *Crusader*, the Allied effort to relieve Tobruk, during late 1941.

An Australian infantry section in service dress, Libya, 1940. At this stage the gas mask was still worn on the chest. (Bettmann/Getty Images)

Italian

By 1938 the Italian Army had adopted *La guerra di rapido corso* ('the war of rapid course') as its official doctrine. This established the use of surprise, speed, intensity, sustained action and the ability to modify a plan in the light of unforeseen contingencies. Italian forces would manoeuvre against the flank of an enemy and use motorized forces to exploit a breakthrough. In the attack, fire would be focused on the weakest enemy defences to assist the rapid break-in to an enemy position to turn his line. The infantry would do this, supported by artillery, which made the coordination of artillery with infantry a priority. Engaging in counter-battery fire was also of importance, as was targeting enemy tanks. Mobility was a fundamental characteristic of the artillery. Tankettes would assist the infantry, with a tankette battalion initially part of the infantry-division organization. The attack would be recklessly pressed; this could not be sustained, however, as officers would soon lose motivation.

The establishment of armoured divisions and the provision of medium tanks in 1938 encouraged the use of armour to penetrate the enemy line, though this would only be considered when defences were deemed light. Instead, holding armoured assets for an exploitation, or countering an enemy tank force, were seen as the tanks' primary tasks. Specialized reconnaissance units to collect information about the enemy were not organized by the time the Desert War began in June 1940. Armoured cars equipped with radios were not prioritized.

Italian doctrine discouraged the adoption of static defensive positions; these were seen as no more than temporary expedients until the offensive could be resumed. The main line of resistance was situated as far as possible from the enemy's artillery with a zone of security 2,000–3,500yd deep established in front of the main line. Holding positions in this zone were to be established in terrain offering cover. The enemy would be worn down along the easiest routes prior to encountering the main line.

The infantry organization based on the binary system was founded on the assumption that the division was only capable of a frontal attack. During the Second Italo-Ethiopian War, while one Italian division fixed the enemy, another would envelop the enemy line or exploit success. Infantry was tasked with the exploitation of a successful attack. If the initial attack failed, poor artillery performance was held responsible, but the artillery was not to blame. The coordination the guns needed with the infantry was only possible with good communications, which were lacking. Observation of a target was essential, though, and this was achieved by positioning the guns forward and sometimes using direct laying onto targets. Italian gunners earned a good reputation for accurate targeting and manning the guns despite facing imminent danger.

Italian infantry deployed to North Africa were organized as either *motorizatta* (motorized) or *semi-transportabile* (semi-motorized) divisions. The majority of infantry assigned to the desert would serve in *divisioni autotransportabile Tipo Africa Settentriole* (North Africa-type motorized divisions) by 1942. This type of formation had about 7,500 men, 52 field and anti-tank guns and 434 lorries and tractors. By comparison, the British infantry division possessed 18,347 men, 120 field and anti-tank guns and 1,657 cars and lorries; the German infantry division had some 13,000 men, 48 field and anti-tank guns and 942 lorries.

Four infantry divisions – 61[a] 'Sirte', 62[a] 'Marmarica', 63[a] 'Cirene' and 64[a] 'Catanzaro' – were destroyed in late 1940 and early 1941. Six others – 16[a] 'Pistoia', 17[a] 'Pavia', 25[a] 'Bologna', 27[a] 'Brescia', 55[a] 'Savona' and 60[a] 'Sabratha' – fought the British during 1941–42. Each, during 1941, theoretically had two infantry regiments each with three infantry battalions. The *reggimento di artiglieria* (artillery regiment) belonging to infantry divisions typically had two 75/27 field-artillery groups (24 guns in total), a single 100/17 gun group (12 guns) and at least one air-defence battery with eight 20mm guns. During 1940 and early 1941, a light-tank battalion with 46 L3/35 tankettes was also part of the organizational structure. Only eight

Pictured in November 1940, this 75/46 modello 34 anti-aircraft gun is being used against ground targets in North Africa. The weapon was frequently used against Allied tanks; its 75mm round could penetrate 3.54in of armour at 550yd. (FPG/Archive Photos/Getty Images)

47/32 anti-tank guns were issued to the division in 1940; these formed a *compagnia cannoni controcarro*. A *battaglione misto del genio* (mixed engineer battalion) and a *battaglione complementi* (replacement battalion) completed the organization.

Both the 'Trieste' and 'Trento' Motorized divisions deployed to North Africa were supposed to possess enough transport to haul their artillery pieces and transport a high proportion of infantry, composed of one regiment of *bersaglieri* and two motorized infantry regiments. By mid-1942, divisional artillery included 24 75/27 field guns, 24 100/17 guns, 12 88mm or 90mm dual-purpose guns and 24 20mm guns. 'Trieste' fought alongside the tanks of the 'Ariete' Armoured Division. An engineer battalion, and transportation, supply and medical detachments completed the organization. By early 1942, 'Trieste' also had a tank battalion with 52 medium tanks and the VIII Battaglione bersaglieri corazzato, an armoured reconnaissance unit. 'Trento' lacked these units and much of its organic transport assets were taken away for use by higher-echelon transportation units. This meant 'Trento' could not accompany the armour on mobile operations.

In theory the infantry regiments sent to North Africa during early 1941 had three *battaglioni fanteria* (infantry battalions), a *compagnia mortai* (mortar company) with six 81mm mortars and a *batteria d'accompagnemento* (gun battery) with four 65/17 guns. An infantry battalion had three infantry companies and a weapons company. Changes during 1941 specified the forming of a *battaglione armi d'accompagnement e controcarri* (anti-tank and support battalion) with a mortar company (nine 81mm mortars), an anti-tank company (eight 47/32 guns) and an air-defence company (eight 20/35 guns) within each infantry regiment. The *divisione motorizzata Africa Settentriole* organization of 1942 established infantry battalions with four companies, each with organic support weapons; the heavy-weapons battalions were dissolved. This organization did not apply to all infantry divisions as the 'Brescia' Infantry Division was excluded.

This soldier's unit is about to assault Australian positions dug in on a reverse slope. A desert veteran, he is apprehensive at the prospect of facing the Australians in combat.

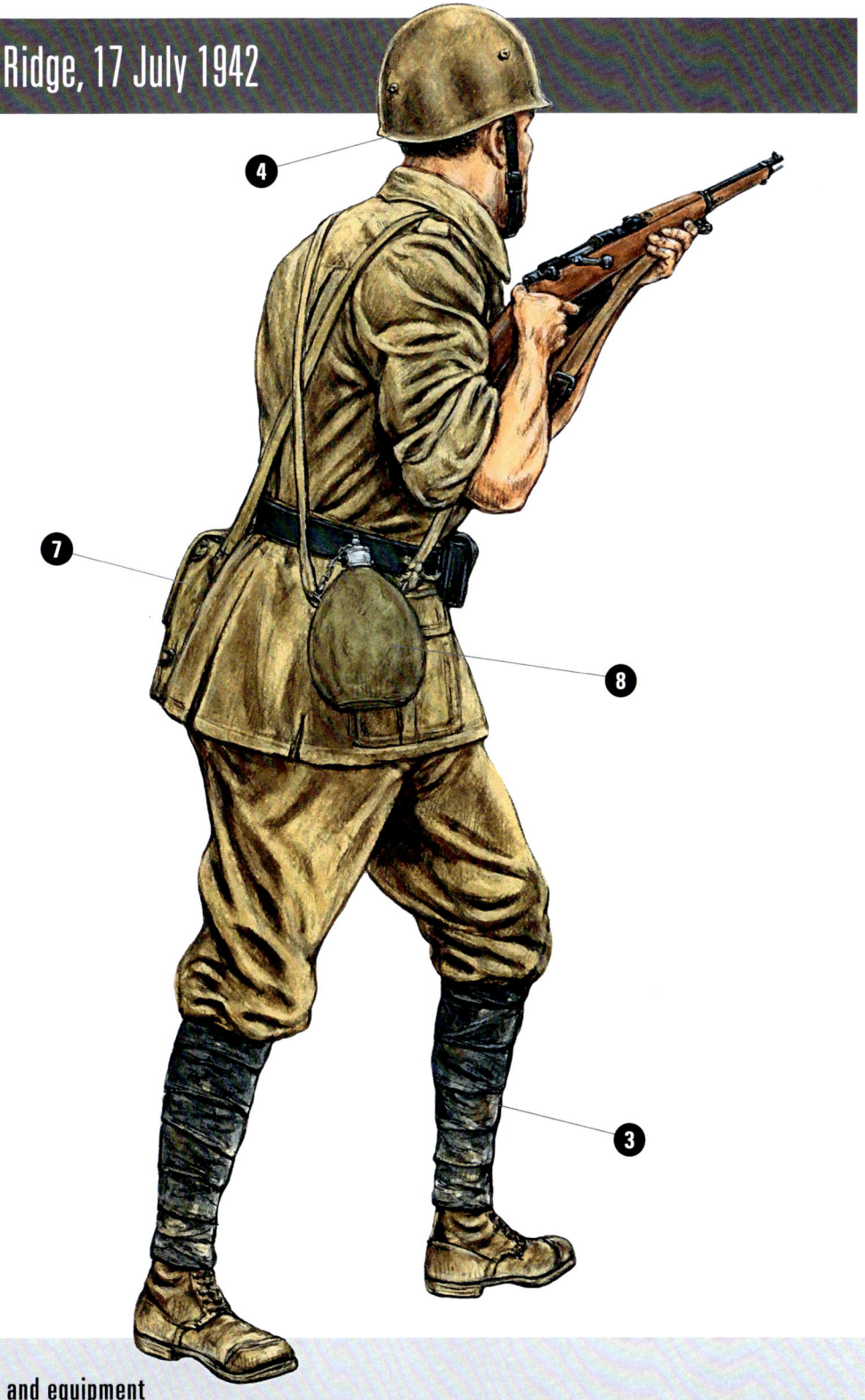

Weapons, dress and equipment

The soldier is armed with a bolt-action M1891/41 Carcano rifle (**1**), firing a 6.5mm bullet. The rifle's integral box magazine holds six bullets, loaded using a clip. He wears a *camiciotto sahariana* smock (**2**). His M41 trousers are tucked into puttees (**3**). He wears an M33 helmet (**4**).

Rifle-ammunition pouches (**5**) supported by straps around his neck are worn at the front of his belt. Hanging from the belt is a scabbard (**6**) carrying his rifle bayonet. Suspended from straps over his shoulders, he wears a haversack (**7**) on his left side and a water bottle (**8**) on his right.

RECRUITMENT, MORALE AND LOGISTICS

Commonwealth

Formerly 127th Queen Mary's Own Baluch Light Infantry, 3/10 Baluch was assigned to 5 Indian Brigade (4th Indian Division) on 18 April 1942. In 1922, five Baluchi regiments were amalgamated into a formation named 10 Baluch Regiment. The 1920s saw changes to the regiment's ethnic make-up, with each battalion receiving a Dogra Brahman company. Officers thought that agricultural Dogra Brahmans were keen to serve and had a sturdy physique (Maxwell 2009· 76). During 1924–29, 3/10 Baluch was stationed near Lahore, defending the North West Frontier. In October 1929 the battalion was sent to occupy Wana, territory lost during the Third Anglo-Afghan War (1919). In 1931 the battalion was sent to Rangoon in Burma.

By 1934, Punjabi Muslims composed half 3/10 Baluch's strength. Recruitment quotas for Muslims were established, with 35 per cent from Rawalpindi, 35 per cent from Jhelum and the remaining 30 per cent from Gujarat, Shahpur, Attock and Mianwali. After returning from Waziristan in September 1940, the battalion sent 100 personnel to form 6/10 and 7/10 Baluch before preparing for overseas service. In January 1941 the Pathan composition (B Coy) was changed; they accounted for one-quarter of the battalion's strength and were composed of one-third Yusufzai and two-thirds Khattaks. This ratio was swapped, resulting in a block to Khattak promotions, though this did not cause lasting problems.

Setting sail in July 1941, 3/10 Baluch was part of 18 Indian Brigade, participating in the occupation of Iran during August. By late autumn the battalion was on its way to Egypt. During December 1941, 3/10 Baluch was at Mersa Matruh, part of 38 Indian Brigade; on 1 January 1942 the brigade was posted to Tobruk, guarding the port until late March when it was ordered to assemble east of El Adem, Libya. In April, the battalion joined 5 Indian Brigade at Kabrit, Egypt, serving alongside 4/6 Rajputana Rifles and 1/4 Essex. Initially sent to Palestine, 5 Indian Brigade was ordered back to the Western Desert on 3 June, departing on 8 June.

On 17 July 1940, 2/43 Battalion was raised at Woodside, South Australia. While the bulk of the enlisted personnel had no military experience, many officers and NCOs had joined the militia first. During July 1940 the men of 2/43 Battalion attended a camp in the Adelaide Hills. Training involved weapons handling, then company and battalion exercises commenced. Platoon training for infantry included observation, patrols, attacking and defending localities; 18 Platoon had only a single Lewis gun and no mortars.

On 28 December, 2/43 Battalion's personnel entrained for Melbourne where they took ship for Ceylon and then Egypt. In February 1941, they began acclimatization training in Palestine. Section and platoon training soon followed, when Bren carriers and motor transport arrived. Time for company- and battalion-level exercises was limited as by mid-March the battalion deployed to Tobruk and remained there for six months. Casualties amounted to 51 killed, 156 wounded and four taken prisoner. By October 1941, the battalion was being rebuilt in Palestine; in January 1942 it was sent to Syria to train with replacements. By June the battalion conducted mobile manoeuvres,

moving in a box formation. Some of the men trained to be part of 'Jock' columns (small combined-arms formations of armour, artillery and infantry; named after Lt-Col J.C. 'Jock' Campbell) and the whole battalion gained experience of working alongside tanks in darkness. Only in June did brigade exercises occur, in the Syrian desert. Late in June the battalion deployed to El Alamein. The first battle for many of the men took place on 7 July.

During January 1940, 21 NZ Battalion formed at Papakura Military Camp, south of Auckland, as part of 5 NZ Brigade; 40 per cent of the men had TA experience, 34 per cent were aged 20–24 and only 10 per cent had rural backgrounds. On 2 May 1940, the battalion departed for Scotland. Deployed to Greece in April 1941, 21 NZ Battalion fought at Platamon on 14 April and Pinios Gorge on 18 April. Elements reached the coast to be taken off by boat, but 230 men were taken prisoner. In late April, 237 soldiers formed the battalion strength on Crete though others joined later. Another 148 casualties were suffered during May when the Germans captured Crete. With 500 replacements joining the 270 survivors, only by August would 21 NZ Battalion train properly.

Casualties suffered by the New Zealanders during Operation *Crusader* in late November 1941 amounted to a staggering 4,620 men. On 10 December, 21 NZ Battalion had 340 new officers and men assigned. During February 1942, 5 NZ Brigade including 21 NZ Battalion practised landings from ships, before being sent to build a defensive box at El Adem. On 10 June, 5 NZ Brigade concentrated for training east of Aleppo when orders took the brigade back to Egypt as Rommel had broken through the Gazala Line.

On 15–16 July, 21 NZ Battalion, less D Coy, fought for Ruweisat Ridge; A Coy and C Coy had to be amalgamated because of losses. From 26 June to early September, the battalion lost 67 killed, 180 wounded and 40 taken prisoner. Training resumed, involving a march through darkness and breaching wire with explosives. The assaulting infantry were to advance behind a creeping artillery barrage. When they reached their objective, supporting arms were to be transported on lorries through gaps in the minefield to the infantry positions.

ABOVE LEFT

A Gurkha soldier armed with an M1928 Thompson SMG wields his kukri, Tunisia, 26 July 1943. Similarly armed troops of the 2/4 Gurkha Rifles served in 10th Indian Division during the battle of Gazala (21 May–21 June 1942). (Associated Press/Alamy Stock Photo)

ABOVE RIGHT

Troops of 28 (Māori) Battalion perform a *haka* (a ceremonial war dance) for King George II of Greece at Helwan, Egypt, 24 July 1941. Only one of the four men in the foreground survived World War II. From left are pictured: John Manuel from Rangitukia, killed on 15 December 1941; Maaka White of Wharekahika, killed on 23 November 1941; Te Kooti Reihana of Rangitukia, subsequently wounded; and Rangi Henderson from Te Araroa, killed on 26 March 1943. (Pictures from History/Universal Images Group via Getty Images)

Italian

Formed in Romagna on 27 April 1939, the 'Pavia' Infantry Division, composed of the 27° and 28° Reggimenti di fanteria, participated in the Axis siege of Tobruk during June 1941. During Operation *Crusader* it helped to contain the extent of the British breakthrough in late November 1941, and served to cover the withdrawal of German and Italian forces.

Formed in Calabria on 27 April 1939, 'Brescia' included the 19° and 20° Reggimenti di fanteria. The artillery regiment, infantry support-weapons companies and the anti-tank company sent to stem the British advance during Operation *Compass* were largely destroyed at Beda Fomm. In February 1941, the 1° Reggimento artiglieria celere disembarked and was attached to 'Brescia'.

The 'Bologna' Infantry Division was formed at Naples on 27 April 1939 with the 39° and 40° Reggimenti di fanteria. 'Bologna' was assigned to the siege of Tobruk in 1941, then withdrew to El Agheila by December 1941, and did not participate in the fighting at Gazala in May–June 1942, instead being brought up to the front only in mid-July.

Of the other infantry divisions, 'Pistoia' deployed during September 1942, on the Egyptian border and did not fight at Second El Alamein. 'Savona' was disbanded during January 1942 when the Italian garrisons in the Sollum–Bardia locality capitulated. Established in 1937, 'Sabratha' was nearly destroyed at Beda Fomm; re-formed by September 1941, it participated in the siege of Tobruk. On 10 July 1942, 26 Australian Brigade routed 'Sabratha', with 1,500 Italians taken prisoner. On 25 July, 'Sabratha' personnel were amalgamated into 'Trento'.

Turning to the motorized infantry divisions, 'Trieste' was formed in 1939 in Piacenza and fought during Operation *Crusader*. The division's separate *battaglione armi d'accompagnemento* was disbanded by September 1941. The limited utility of the lorries would limit the operational possibilities of 'Trieste'. The lack of armoured vehicles to transport the infantry meant they had to approach on foot, lengthening the time they were exposed to enemy artillery fire. By the end of Operation *Crusader*, losses meant both the 65° and 66° Reggimenti fanteria motorizzato had lost their support-weapons battalions and had only a single 81mm mortar company each. Although 'Trieste' lost its *bersaglieri* permanently on 29 March 1942, the division now had a tank battalion and a *bersaglieri* armoured battalion. The ratio of guns to infantry was higher. With these

Italian weapons pits, Libya, 1941. The nearest gun team have a Breda 20/65 modello 35 anti-aircraft gun firing from a low silhouette; the Italian infantry used this weapon against ground targets although it was intended for air defence. The pit beyond it has a Breda 30 LMG. (Fireshot Studio/Fototeca/Universal Images Group via Getty Images)

changes the formation could operate semi-autonomously. While theoretical strength was supposed to be 6,671, only 5,197 men could be deployed for the fighting at Gazala.

Formed in 1939, 'Trento' deployed to North Africa during March 1941 and was converted to a Type 42 formation beginning in September that year. On 29 December it lost the 7° Reggimento bersaglieri, but was not allocated a tank battalion. By October 1942, each of the two infantry regiments had three battalions and an 81mm mortar company.

The Italian formations fighting in North Africa did not possess enough motor transport, because Italian industry lacked the capacity to replace the vehicle losses suffered during the Ethiopian and Spanish conflicts. A limited number of vehicles, mainly SPA 38R light trucks and Lancia 3Ro lorries, was available. The SPA 38R had a high fuel consumption rate and a range of 180 miles, with a load capacity of 2.5 tons or 25 men. The Lancia 3Ro was better, with a load capacity of 6.3 tons or 42 men. A chronic lack of fuel also influenced transport capability, with battlefield mobility impaired by petrol and oil shortages.

Newly arrived Italian reinforcements pictured during training in Tripolitania, March 1942. As Italy was largely an agrarian society, most men joining the Army had peasant backgrounds. The military training law of 1925 established the teaching of basic military knowledge and weapons handling for men aged 18–21. When aged 21, men fit for service (about 75 per cent) joined the Army. Conscripts served for 1–1½ years and then stayed on the active list for ten years. (Mondadori via Getty Images)

WEAPONS, TRAINING AND TACTICS

Commonwealth

Commonwealth infantrymen used weapons Britain procured during the interwar years for Imperial policing operations – accurate, light weapons designed for marksmen who would not expend excessive amounts of ammunition. The rifle section, by April 1942 composed of nine men including its leader, was the core of the infantry. Commanded by a corporal usually armed with a .45 M1928 Thompson SMG, it had a manoeuvre element composed of riflemen and a fire element based on the .303 Bren LMG. The Bren-gun team was commanded by the assistant section leader, a lance corporal, and included a gunner and a rifleman who carried six Bren magazines. Each soldier of the rifle group also carried two Bren magazines.

The rifle or assault group of six men was commanded by the section leader and sought to close with the enemy to throw grenades at his position. Capable of firing 15rd/min and with an effective range of 550yd, the .303 SMLE Mk III bolt-action rifle was the standard infantry weapon. The .45 M1928 Thompson SMG carried by many section leaders could be fitted with a 20-round stick magazine or a 50-round drum magazine, but the latter was unpopular due to its weight and unwieldiness in combat. Though the Bren's use of a magazine limited the rate of fire, misfires were rare because the ammunition was kept clean. The frequency of barrel changes was low because a low rate of fire reduced the problem of overheating.

The rifle platoon was composed of three rifle sections and a 2in mortar team often accompanying the platoon sergeant, although by the middle of 1942 the mortars were issued to HQ Coy and not the rifle platoons. When attacking, the platoon commander would use a rifle section to provide suppressing fire, while a rifle section closed with the enemy position. Another rifle section would be used on an enveloping manoeuvre to stop the enemy

withdrawing or to prevent reinforcements from getting to the position being assaulted. The mortar crew used smoke or high-explosive rounds against enemy positions. The 2in mortar weighed 10.5lb and had a range of 500yd; the rate of fire was 8rd/min.

A Commonwealth infantry battalion's carrier platoon had 13 carriers and was used to offer protection to Bren-gun teams to move to a good firing position. Middle East establishments provided each carrier with a Bren gun, an anti-tank rifle and a rifleman equipped with a rifle-grenade discharger. By 1942 each carrier section had a radio to communicate with the rifle company it was supporting.

Most Lee-Enfield rifles used by the Indian formations were manufactured at Ishapore; the factory there produced 600,000 during World War II. The first Indian battalions to deploy to the Middle East lacked anti-tank guns, even in 1941. Despite possessing only one anti-tank gun, 3 Motor Brigade managed to hold the Germans for 48 hours at Mechili in April 1941 to enable the Australians to get to Tobruk before the Germans. In June 1942, 5 Indian Brigade had eight 2-pdr anti-tank guns allocated to each battalion only one week prior to battle.

Deployed to Tobruk without any mortars, carriers or grenades, 2/43 Battalion used captured Italian weapons, notably 47/32 anti-tank guns. Platoon headquarters received mortars by the end of 1941, and the battalion got its own MMG platoon during August 1942.

On 3 January 1941, 21 NZ Battalion sailed for Egypt, and disembarked at Port Tewfik on 3 March. On 22 April, 2nd NZ Division commenced a four-day exercise in the desert. This was such a fiasco that Freyberg mandated his battalion commanders to teach a training syllabus based on the War Office's Military Training Pamphlet No. 37, 'The Training of an Infantry Battalion'. On 28 September, 19 NZ Battalion participated in an exercise with Bren-gun carriers and tanks; the infantry was 200yd behind in trucks and debussed when the tanks engaged targets, though no enemy fire was being experienced.

ABOVE LEFT
A New Zealand 25-pdr field-gun crew undertakes night firing in Libya, 28 July 1942. The 25-pdr was the standard gun equipping Commonwealth divisional artillery regiments. Each of the three artillery regiments of 2nd NZ Infantry Division operated three batteries each of eight guns. Range was 13,400yd. At El Alamein on 24 October 1942, the artillery used a creeping barrage technique, much to the displeasure of Major-General Tuker, GOC 4th Indian Division. (Associated Press/Alamy Stock Photo)

ABOVE RIGHT
An Eighth Army artillery crew with a 5.5in medium gun, 3 August 1942. Capable of firing a 100lb shell 16,200yd, this gun made its combat debut on the El Alamein battlefield. (Associated Press/Alamy Stock Photo)

Italian

Italian tactics placed emphasis upon fire rather than manoeuvre. For infantry to advance on enemy defences, suppressive fire from MMGs was seen as necessary. Narrow frontages of 50yd for a platoon and 400yd for a battalion were used, leading to high numbers of casualties. This approach made superiority of numbers the principal characteristic of Italian tactics. If the initial attack was unsuccessful, additional forces would be committed. A lack of off-road mobility and logistics discouraged the adoption of enveloping manoeuvres. Poor leadership stopped the Italian troops from using infiltration tactics. It was believed that while defending, firepower would win the day; the use of counter-attacks was not a priority. This meant Italian defences were brittle; when ammunition ran low they could easily be defeated. A lack of motor transport meant ammunition resupply was not certain.

The two light machine guns belonging to the rifle squad could alternate fire and movement. The rifle group adjusted its movement according to the LMG firing. When within 30–40yd of an enemy position, the riflemen were tasked with the final assault by throwing grenades. The commander of the squad led the assault. During this final assault the LMG teams would advance because firing would be too dangerous, potentially hitting the rifle squad. The assault was implemented by both squads, each composed of two NCOs and 16 soldiers. While occupying defensive positions, the squad commander sited his LMGs so they could coordinate fire. A security zone would be used; the most threatening enemy would be targeted by the LMGs sited in this zone and then on order from the platoon commander, the squad would withdraw on a route known to other defenders by means of leaps and bounds to a designated position. The squad's complement of riflemen was divided in two and deployed on the wings of the LMG's position. The deputy squad commander looked after the provision of ammunition. The platoon commander coordinated the movements of both of his squads. By early 1942, the squad had nine soldiers and two NCOs, and the platoon had a single infantry squad, an MMG squad, an anti-tank rifle squad and an anti-tank gun section. This emphasis on support weapons limited the options for using infantry for assaults.

Equipment was designed to perform the roles doctrine specified. The 6.5mm Carcano modello 1891 was the bolt-action rifle used by Italian infantry; but a low bullet velocity meant the rifle was not the best. An internal magazine holding six rounds was used. The 6.5mm Fucile Mitragliatore Breda modello 30 was the standard LMG used by the infantry. The weapon was of poor design, however. In North Africa the Breda 30's fully automatic mode of firing was not practical because rounds got stuck so often. The weapon was on semi-automatic most of the time and this made a rate of fire with reloading of 60rd/min the standard. An LMG team was made up of a corporal gunner, assistant gunner and two ammunition bearers. Experienced NCOs were nominated as machine-gunners because of the difficulties of using the weapon. The officers knew the deficiencies and made sure every soldier was trained to load ammunition into the magazine.

The 8mm Mitragliatrica Breda modello 37 was the standard MMG used by the infantry. The ammunition did not need oiling, though the use of 20-

round trays of cartridges limited the rate of fire. The weapon was air-cooled so it could not be continuously fired anyway. Up to 200rd/min could be fired if the loader fed in ammunition trays continuously. The Breda 37 was popular with the infantry, though it weighed 83lb with tripod. Effective firing range was 875–1,100yd.

By mid-1942 most Italian infantry no longer used the 45mm mortar; instead they used the 81mm mortar. The 45mm mortar had a rate of fire of 8–10rd/min and a range of 580yd. Ignition cartridges had to be fed into a special magazine for the trigger to work. Fragmentation was poor and the low calibre limited effectiveness. The 81/14 Modello 35 mortar weighed 131lb and could fire either a light bomb out to 2.5 miles or a heavy bomb out to 1 mile. Rate of fire was up to 18rd/min.

The artillery was considered the finest branch of the Italian Army. Most of the guns used dated from World War I, however, and were outclassed by newer models. The use of 75mm guns by most of the artillery groups placed the infantry at some disadvantage as the Germans had issued 10.5cm guns to their artillery battalions. The 65/17 gun issued to the gun battery of infantry regiments had a range of 7,400yd. The 47/32 anti-tank gun was a capable weapon, but by 1942 was outclassed by the British 6-pdr anti-tank gun. The German 3.7cm anti-tank gun was issued to some Italian infantry formations. Used to engage aircraft and ground targets, the 20/65 Breda modello 35 gun could be mounted on vehicles or trailers; it could penetrate 1.18in of armour at a range of 550yd.

COMMAND, CONTROL AND COMMUNICATIONS

Commonwealth

British Army officers needed character; selection boards stressed courage and physical fitness, with high intelligence last on the list of required attributes. Pay was poor, at 10s a day; enough to pay mess fees but little else, which was why many poorer officers decided to go to India as living costs there were much lower. Lieutenant-General Montgomery did not think much of Indian Army officers, however, probably seeing as detrimental the doctrinal influence of Major-General T.W. Corbett, formerly Chief of Staff, Middle East. In October 1942, Montgomery did not give 4th Indian Division much of a role during Second El Alamein. Major-General F.I.S. Tuker, GOC 4th Indian Division, would convince him otherwise in future operations.

Through World War I, the only Indian officers were Viceroy Commissioned Officers (VCOs). Only Indian soldiers had to salute them and the British saw them as a type of warrant officer. By 1918, Indian officer cadets attended Royal Military College Sandhurst. During 1918–26, 85 cadets passed through, graduating as King Commissioned Indian Officers (KCIOs); 25 failed to graduate. India founded a military academy of its own at Dehradun; the first Indian cadets commenced their studies there on 10 December 1932. Each year, 80 officer cadets began a 2½-year course, one year longer than the RMC Sandhurst course; they graduated as Indian Commissioned Officers (ICOs). By 1939, about 600 KCIOs and ICOs were part of the Indian Army. By then the course at Dehradun lasted only 18 months. Dehradun had passed out 290 officers by 1939, though training was basic and lacked technical skills. When posted to their battalions, Indian officers did not socialize with British officers. Many officers were still British. This was not a problem; if the Indian soldier thought the British officer the right kind, then he would go through thick and thin for him.

Lieutenant-Colonel A.C. Taylor, CO 3/10 Baluch, permitted his company commanders and staff a lot of leeway as long as they told him what was going on. He had a reputation of being a difficult person to fool and could see through any smokescreen of excuses. Taylor was seen to be strict and fair; his officers found him sympathetic and ready with sound advice. On deployment from India, Captain J.F. Robinson commanded HQ Coy. A Coy was composed of Punjabi Muslims and was commanded by Captain A. Hamid Khan. B Coy was composed of Pathans and was commanded by Captain J.M. Forster. C Coy, composed of Dogra Brahmans, and D Coy, composed of Punjabi Muslims, were both commanded by second lieutenants. Seven emergency commissioned officers who had joined since war broke out accompanied the battalion; six Subadar and 16 Jemadar VCOs also held command roles.

The Commonwealth divisional formations had a distinctive relationship with higher-formation commanders. If they thought an operation too risky they could ask their government at home to intercede with the British government to stop them participating. This applied to the Australians and New Zealanders, but Indian commanding officers did not opt to use this approach. Major-General Freyberg, the New Zealand divisional commander, was an experienced soldier who could refuse to see any of his brigades detached from his formation. He successfully argued for 4 Armoured Brigade to be attached to his 2nd NZ Division during Operation *Crusader*. During October 1942 the New Zealanders were assigned 9 Armoured Brigade.

The issue of whether an operation was too risky or not was pertinent because a mistake might see whole brigades destroyed as fighting formations if enemy armour wreaked havoc. The lack of control at the higher echelons of command was obvious to many Commonwealth commanders. The inability of British armour to work closely to protect the infantry appeared to indicate a faulty command style stemming from the selection and promotion of officers. The training they received at staff college aggravated the situation. Staff college was not a military think tank tasked with developing doctrine; instead, syndicates discussed tactical problems then agreed upon solutions. A collegiate approach to command was inculcated. Places were filled by nominations made by commanding officers and not by examination. The consensual command style was a ponderous safety-first mode, hampering effective decision-making. Plans could be knocked off course by assessments – frequently wrong – of the enemy's situation based on the interpretation of intercepted enemy messages.

Montgomery detested the consensual style of leadership. He refused to allow any dilution of orders by subordinates. He sought to stage-manage a battle, train for it and maintain the aim. He explained why it was being fought and gave the men the means to do it. He would not respond to the enemy's movements; instead, he would maintain his own aim. His experience was of training a citizen army manned with conscripts who responded to a personal approach. His appointment was fortuitous because the first choice for command of Eighth Army, Lieutenant-General W.H.E. Gott, was killed on 7 August 1942 near Alexandria, Egypt, when the aircraft he was travelling in was forced down and then strafed by Luftwaffe fighters.

Telephones were relied upon in defensive positions. Runners could be used to communicate between company headquarters and the platoons. A radio link from brigade to battalion was the best that could be expected until 1942, when some companies began to be equipped with radios. On the battlefield the infantry battalion's signals platoon operated a No. 18 radio set from late 1941. This enabled the battalion commander to keep in touch with his four rifle-company commanders and the commanders of the mortar and carrier platoons. These radios, worn on the back or mounted on a carrier, had to be tuned to the same frequency to communicate with each other. The battalion headquarters set was the control set communicating the selected frequency to the other sets. By early 1942, nine sets were allocated to each

Captain Charles H. Upham, one of only three people to be awarded the Victoria Cross twice, is pictured eating with soldiers of 20 NZ Battalion in 1942. TA personnel, usually from the educated middle classes, made up the majority of the 1,000 officers needed for 2nd NZ Division. They attended a week's course at Trentham, near Wellington, firing the Lewis LMG, using a compass, learning infantry drill, tactics and organization and then obtained a commission. (Universal History Archive/Getty Images)

infantry battalion. Range was 2–5 miles with a 6ft aerial, or up to 10 miles with a 10ft aerial.

The No. 38 radio set was used by soldiers other than signallers; it was lighter and issued to platoon commanders. Range was 0.75 miles with a 4ft aerial or up to 12 miles with a 12ft aerial. By the summer of 1942, 30 sets were theoretically on the establishment of each infantry battalion. The Commonwealth infantry platoon did not operate with these sets during First and Second El Alamein, however.

Italian

Officers approached training with a distant and formal attitude towards the enlisted soldier. No sense of comradeship was felt between officers and men. Junior reserve officers who conducted training had little knowledge of modern tactical techniques; and the Italian Army did not possess enough senior NCOs as few conscripts decided to make the military a career. Pay was low, benefits poor and prospects upon leaving undefined. Senior officers mostly had administrative roles or taught officer cadets. The ratio of NCOs to privates was 1:33. The training of *bersaglieri* and gunners was better, though, because they had superior NCOs and officers.

Regular infantry officers attended the Modena Military Academy for two years, then spent another year in a specialist military school if infantry or cavalry, two years if artillerymen or engineers. The number of junior officers was insufficient because a financial crisis forced the Army to dismiss half of its lieutenants during the mid-1920s. Military academies then had to guarantee a permanent commission to second lieutenants. This led the Army to use reservist officers to command platoons, companies and gun batteries; but most of them had served during the 1930s and had not seen combat. Older reserve officers were made captains if they had seen service in the late 1920s or early 1930s. Those who had participated during World War I were made majors or lieutenant-colonels. The training needed to promote a reservist lieutenant to captain was limited. The best reservist officers were sent to train new conscripts. During 1939–40, battalions might possess only a handful of regular officers. Superior officers tended to supervise juniors too closely and this, along with the older demographic of reservists, tended to discourage initiative.

Conscript officers who met certain educational standards received seven months' instruction as cadets. They would probably be sent with no combat experience to North Africa. Senior officers had probably spent time in Libya prior to the war and had some knowledge of the problems of a desert environment.

Command was decentralized, with platoon commanders using initiative during offensives. Some officers believed that courage, rather than training, would see the soldier succeed. It was a commonly held belief that on-the-job training would be the best preparation for infantry. Promotions for officers were by seniority; pay and benefits were high. Junior-officer training lost out, however, which meant senior officers had to watch them closely. Senior officers did not get retired; instead, they had other appointments to go to as the number of units expanded. The high expenditure on officers meant less money could be spent on weapons.

Italian and German officers confer, Tobruk, August 1941. The Germans thought the British slow and clumsy; they exhibited no initiative and could not alter tactics if battle developed in a way they did not expect. A lack of unit cooperation was noticed. Tank units were slow to exploit opportunities. Anti-tank guns were not used in the assault. The infantry was the most effective element and it proved difficult to put them to flight. Tough and determined, they would withdraw according to plan, or defend positions until annihilated or captured. (Mondadori via Getty Images)

Generale d'armata Roatta conducted a wartime study of Army officers. He highlighted timidity, inadequate technical knowledge, poor understanding of radio equipment, poor map reading and compass use, lack of knowledge of field fortifications, poor physical conditioning and total administrative ignorance as their primary deficits. From mid-1941 he established that officer candidates had to take a demanding sergeant's course, serve as NCOs for two or three months with a unit stationed in Italy, and then complete a realistic officer training course. Junior officers on the course had to deal with tactical problems and solve them quickly with practical solutions.

He made some efforts to correct these issues among junior officers, but none with senior officers. The older age of senior officers perhaps meant changes to doctrine were difficult to enforce, for a certain intellectual rigidity encouraged a lack of curiosity. The worst offenders were middle-ranking officers from reserve forces. Generale d'armata Bastico noticed they lacked energy, while Generale Claudio Trezzani was also scathing about junior officers, observing that as long as it was a question of being brave they had no problem, but when they had to make battlefield decisions they were hopeless – and when they had to scout ahead, close with the enemy, conduct preparatory fire and coordinate movement they were illiterate.

Signal communications was the function of engineers, with the landline heavily relied upon. The Germans particularly bemoaned the lack of Italian radio equipment. Poor communications links with subordinates meant the latter were poorly informed about friendly forces. By 1942, the radio company of a motorized division had a telegraph section, a motor-transported telegraph section, and a radiotelegraph section. The radiotelegraph section had one type R5, two type R4, two type R4-A, nine type RF3C, two type RI2 and two type RA2 radios. Six special radio lorries, and eight lorries with specialist motorcycles transported the equipment. The RF4 was a portable field set for use by the infantry regiments. Four cases and two chests for batteries carried the components. The radio transmitted between 212MHz and 1,550MHz in three bands. Range was 6.2–12.4 miles on R/T and 37–75 miles on continuous wave (Morse). The RF3C was transported by motorcycle to accompany motorized forces. It could transmit between 1.875MHz and 2.5MHz with a range of 12–30 miles.

Ruweisat Ridge

15 July 1942

BACKGROUND TO BATTLE

At first, Rommel's decision to move eastwards towards the Nile River brought him success. At this time, 10th Indian and 50th (Northumbrian) Infantry divisions held Mersa Matruh with 1st Armoured Division and 2nd NZ Division to the south; 5 Indian Brigade stood on the southern approaches, while 2nd NZ Division was nearby at Minqar Qaim, on the Sidi Hamza escarpment, with 29 Indian Brigade. Further south, 1st Armoured Division was ordered to halt a German approach around Mersa Matruh. Rommel sent his armour south of Mersa Matruh. The Deutsches Afrikakorps with only 63 tanks enveloped Mersa Matruh; instead of attempting to cut off the weak German penetration, the British decided to withdraw to the El Alamein position.

Lieutenant-Colonel Taylor's 3/10 Baluch had departed Palestine in early June 1942 with 5 Indian Brigade. On 19 June, 5 Indian Brigade was ordered to join 10th Indian Division at Sollum. Ordered to withdraw to Mersa Matruh, 5 Indian Brigade covered 125 miles in 48 hours, reaching the destination on 25 June.

Taylor's intention prior to the order to withdraw from Mersa Matruh was to march south for 4 miles then east to cover a gap in the minefields to defend Mersa Matruh. On 27 June, Captain Hamid Khan's A Coy was on the right, Captain Forster's B Coy was on the left, and Captain Chatterji's C Coy was behind them, followed by the Carrier Platoon; the battalion had sent D Coy and non-essential transport, commanded by Major Robinson, back to Amariya. When the march commenced, 1/4 Essex was spotted, held up by enemy fire. Approaching from further east, 3/10 Baluch could see motor columns on a ridge 1,600yd distant. Told wrongly that these were British

columns, the Carrier Platoon approached and was taken under fire, losing 51 men; 3/10 Baluch dug in.

On the morning of 28 June, Taylor was informed that Mersa Matruh was surrounded and that 3/10 Baluch needed to break out. Once it was dark, the battalion moved on lorries up the ridge known to be occupied by enemy forces. Only when the battalion reached the height did the German guns hit them, turning some lorries into burning infernos; the others charged on through the gun line. The carriers targeted enemy anti-tank guns; though no carrier made it through unscathed, they distracted attention from the lorries transporting the infantry. Taylor's detour through the desert succeeded in getting his battalion to El Alamein.

At the end of June 1942, 18 Indian Brigade occupied positions at Deir el Shein, to the north-west of Ruweisat Ridge, south-west of the El Alamein box. On 1 July, Rommel (promoted to *Generalfeldmarschall* on 22 June) struck Deir el Shein with the 15. and 21. Panzer-Divisionen; unsupported by 22 Armoured Brigade, 18 Indian Brigade was destroyed, with 2,000 of its men taken prisoner and 30 tanks lost, though the Indians accounted for 18 German tanks. By the end of the day, Rommel had only 54 tanks operational, but he was determined to continue. On 2 July he attempted to surround the El Alamein box but failed. By day's end he had only 26 tanks left. Major-General H.W. Lumsden, GOC 1st Armoured Division, wanted his division to be relieved. Deemed unable to manage Lumsden, Lieutenant-General C.W.M. Norrie was replaced as GOC XXX Corps by Major-General W.H.C. Ramsden, formerly GOC 50th (Northumbrian) Infantry Division.

Indian troops wearing Pattern 1908 gear practise bayonet drill, 1942. During the 1930s, Indian Army infantry platoons were equipped with a single Lewis LMG and no mortars. From 1939, though, when a battalion had orders to go abroad it would be deluged with weapons: 50 LMGs, 6–22 anti-tank rifles and 4–12 2in mortars. A carrier platoon with ten carriers and 65 motor vehicles would accompany each battalion. (The Statesman, Calcutta/Keystone/Hulton Archive/Getty Images)

Aware that Italian formations protected Rommel's southern flank, British forces launched a counter-attack from the south. On 3 July the 'Ariete' Armoured Division, with only eight tanks operational, was assaulted by 4 NZ Brigade and lost its artillery component. Then 5 NZ Brigade headed for El Mreir, a 50ft northern escarpment south-west of the western end of Ruweisat Ridge. On 4 July, elements of the 'Brescia' Infantry Division and the 9° Reggimento bersaglieri forced 21 NZ Battalion back. Rommel then brought his armour south to attack Bab el Qattara on 8 July, though 6 NZ Brigade had withdrawn from the box. Naqb Abu Dweis was also evacuated. The British focused Rommel's attention northward when 9th Australian Division assaulted Italian positions near the coast on 10 July.

During July, the British sought to wear down the Italians because the Germans could not maintain long fronts without them. The operation against Ruweisat Ridge on 15 July, though, was also designed to break the Axis line. Gott's XIII Corps was to seize Point 63 and then exploit to the north-west. The written order to XIII Corps, though, made mention of a consolidation operation. Ordered to protect the New Zealanders' flanks from first light on 15 July, 1st Armoured Division was to exploit to the north-west only if a favourable opportunity presented itself.

The Indians were told only within the final 24 hours that they would participate in the attack, with 5 Indian Brigade, part of XXX Corps, given separate orders. Ramsden ordered 5 Indian Brigade to take the eastern end of the ridge and Point 64. He also set the Indian line back 1 mile on the left though this was 1.5 miles ahead of the New Zealanders' right. Through an error, the Indian line also projected 500yd beyond the New Zealanders' boundary. Because the Indians' operations order only arrived with the New Zealanders when the battle commenced, these discrepancies were not fully appreciated at first.

A convoy of *bersaglieri* on motorcycles move along a Libyan road. While motorcycles provided the *bersaglieri* with good mobility on open ground, they were less effective on open ground. (ullstein bild/ullstein bild via Getty Images)

The New Zealanders thought the purpose of the operation was to seize the ridge so the armour could go round its western end to exploit. If exploitation was not possible they thought each New Zealand brigade would be supported by a brigade of armour. Brigadier H.K. Kippenberger, OC 5 NZ Brigade, doubted that the armour force would support his men quickly; he would be proved right. Both 2 and 22 Armoured brigades were instructed by the divisional order only to prepare to move from first light on 15 July. While 2 Armoured Brigade had orders to exploit success or guard the New Zealanders from Axis tanks, 22 Armoured Brigade was told only to guard against enemy armour, not to exploit success. Artillery support on the ridge when captured by the New Zealanders would also be lacking because the guns would not be close enough.

While 5 NZ Brigade stood on the right, 4 NZ Brigade stood on the left; 5 Indian Brigade was to the right of the New Zealanders. The ridge was to be captured by 0430hrs. On 5 Indian Brigade's right,

3/10 Baluch had orders to seize the ridge; 4/6 Rajputana Rifles on the brigade left had orders to take and hold Point 64, while 1/4 Essex was tasked with mopping-up operations. Support arms, including anti-tank guns, would be brought forward at first light once these objectives were achieved to defend against the suspected counter-attack.

Brigadier Kippenberger bemoaned the lack of artillery support and shortage of information on enemy defences. No single commander was appointed. No coordinating conference was held. Tank support was not available during the attack. On 30 June, 18 Indian Brigade had attempted to entrench on the ridge but could not because of the rocky ground. This information did not reach the New Zealanders or the Indians. No patrols or aerial reconnaissance photographs had identified the copious number of Axis positions forward of the ridge, but 5 Indian Brigade had identified the 'Brescia' and 'Pavia' Infantry divisions on the ridge. A lack of Allied reconnaissance made the intelligence picture confusing. The British expected the enemy to use tanks. The operations order for 1st Armoured Division noted that the 15. Panzer-Division had 35 tanks north of Point 63. The Indians thought the same. In fact, 13 Axis tanks were stationed on the southern slopes of Ruweisat Ridge, on 5 NZ Brigade's approach route. Another company's worth were north of the ridge.

The Italians had ten infantry battalions, two battalions of *bersaglieri*, eight artillery groups and two heavy-artillery groups on the ridge. 'Pavia' with 9° Reggimento bersaglieri was astride the ridge facing east and would engage the Indians. 'Brescia' was south of the ridge facing south and would face the New Zealanders. 'Pavia' had the II/28° Reggimento di fanteria and the 9° Reggimento bersaglieri (XXVIII and XXX Battaglioni) in the first line and the II/27° Reggimento di fanteria and the I/28° Reggimento di fanteria in the second line. Late on 15 July, the III/27° Reggimento di fanteria was assigned to take the place of the XXVIII Battaglione bersaglieri. 'Brescia' deployed four battalions on the front line with only one company in the second line. The 1° Reggimento artiglieria celere with three groups and the 26° Reggimento artiglieria with two groups assisted both formations. The battalions had a total of 4,000 men; each battalion on the first defence line controlled 1,500–2,000m (1,640–2,190yd) of line.

The Italians were supported by 15. Panzer-Division elements, mainly the tanks as most of the German infantry was detached to the 90. leichte Afrika-Division south of the ridge. On 14 July, only 18 German tanks were operational; the 21. Panzer-Division was positioned further north of the ridge. German combat engineers also began laying 9,000 anti-tank mines.

An Italian crew with a German-manufactured 37mm anti-tank gun during the fighting at El Alamein, June–July 1942. While the Italians had good fields of fire during the Ruweisat Ridge fighting on 15–17 July, this advantage was neutralized by the darkness. The Italian guns did not open up in time because they had no notice of the attack. Many gunners were overrun. No supporting artillery bombardment had indicated to the Italians that the attack was under way. (ullstein bild/ullstein bild via Getty Images)

MAP KEY

1 **0000hrs, 15 July:** With C Coy on the right, D Coy and two platoons of B Coy on the left and A Coy in reserve with battalion headquarters, 3/10 Baluch commences its transit through the limited minefields. The XXVIII Battaglione bersaglieri is taken by surprise as it is about to withdraw and be replaced by the III/27° Reggimento di fanteria.

2 **0300hrs, 15 July:** 4/6 Rajputana Rifles is held up by the XXX Battaglione bersaglieri on the forward slope of the ridge.

3 **0400hrs, 15 July:** Having gone further onto the northern slope of the ridge and engaged the II/27° Reggimento di fanteria, elements of A Coy, 21 NZ Battalion, decide to withdraw. On the way down from the ridge the New Zealanders encounter a large Italian strongpoint, probably occupied by the XXX Battaglione bersaglieri, and take it, thereby assisting the Indians' approach.

4 **0600hrs, 15 July:** In the dawn light, Lieutenant-Colonel Taylor sees that 4/6 Rajputana Rifles are pinned down and orders D Coy, 3/10 Baluch, around in support. D Coy takes Point 64, but is forced back by mortar fire from the II/28° Reggimento di fanteria.

5 **0700hrs, 15 July:** 22 NZ Battalion is assaulted by a German tank company situated on the southern slope of the ridge. Positioned near the battalion, Brigadier Kippenberger, OC 5 NZ Brigade, escapes and urges Major-General Lumsden to get his tanks going.

6 **1000hrs, 15 July:** Italian positions are fired upon by the 75mm guns of 9 Lancers (2 Armoured Brigade).

7 **1000–1200hrs, 15 July:** Positions held by the II/27° Reggimento di fanteria are rendered impractical by the assault on Point 64 mounted by D Coy, 3/10 Baluch. Coupled with the losses sustained by the XXX Battaglione bersaglieri, this Indian success assists 4/6 Rajputana Rifles and the battalion gets moving again.

8 **1400–1430hrs, 15 July:** Contact is made between 9 Lancers and 4/6 Rajputana Rifles; the Allied assault defeats the final Italian defences standing firm on the southern slope of the ridge.

9 **1730hrs, 15 July:** German forces recapture Point 63 from 4 NZ Brigade, which is largely destroyed; elements of 5 NZ Brigade, with tanks and Indian forces nearby, manage to escape.

Battlefield environment

El Alamein is a small railway station on the Egyptian coast, 143 miles from Cairo. Some 37 miles south lies the Qattara Depression, impassable ground containing salt marshes. Escarpments stood to the north of the depression. Then the ground consisted of *deir* (shallow depressions), *tell* (summits of little hills) and some rocky ridges running mostly parallel with the coast. These latter features had tactical significance. The El Alamein gap was seen to be a good defence position as early as 1941.

Defence boxes had been established at El Alamein on the coast; at Bab el Qattara, in the middle of the gap; and Naqb Abu Dweis, on the edge of Qattara. While 1st South African Division elements occupied the El Alamein box, 6 NZ Brigade of 2nd NZ Division held Bab el Qattara, with 9 Indian Brigade

at Naqb Abu Dweis. Other brigades held outside boxes would be used as mobile units. The boxes needed armour to stop the Axis forces from bypassing them. Lieutenant-General C.W.M. Norrie, GOC XXX Corps, thought Ruweisat Ridge was essential to stopping the enemy, so 22 Armoured Brigade was positioned on the eastern end. The narrow ridge with good lines of sight was 200ft high and ran east-to-west for 5 miles. The ridge was solid rock, making entrenching difficult, so Eighth Army had stationed infantry at Deir el Shein to the north of the ridge. When the Germans took this position on 1 July, the Italians kept guns to the north guarded by infantry and dug positions on the southern slope. On 15 July, the assaulting Indians did not know the southern slope was so heavily defended.

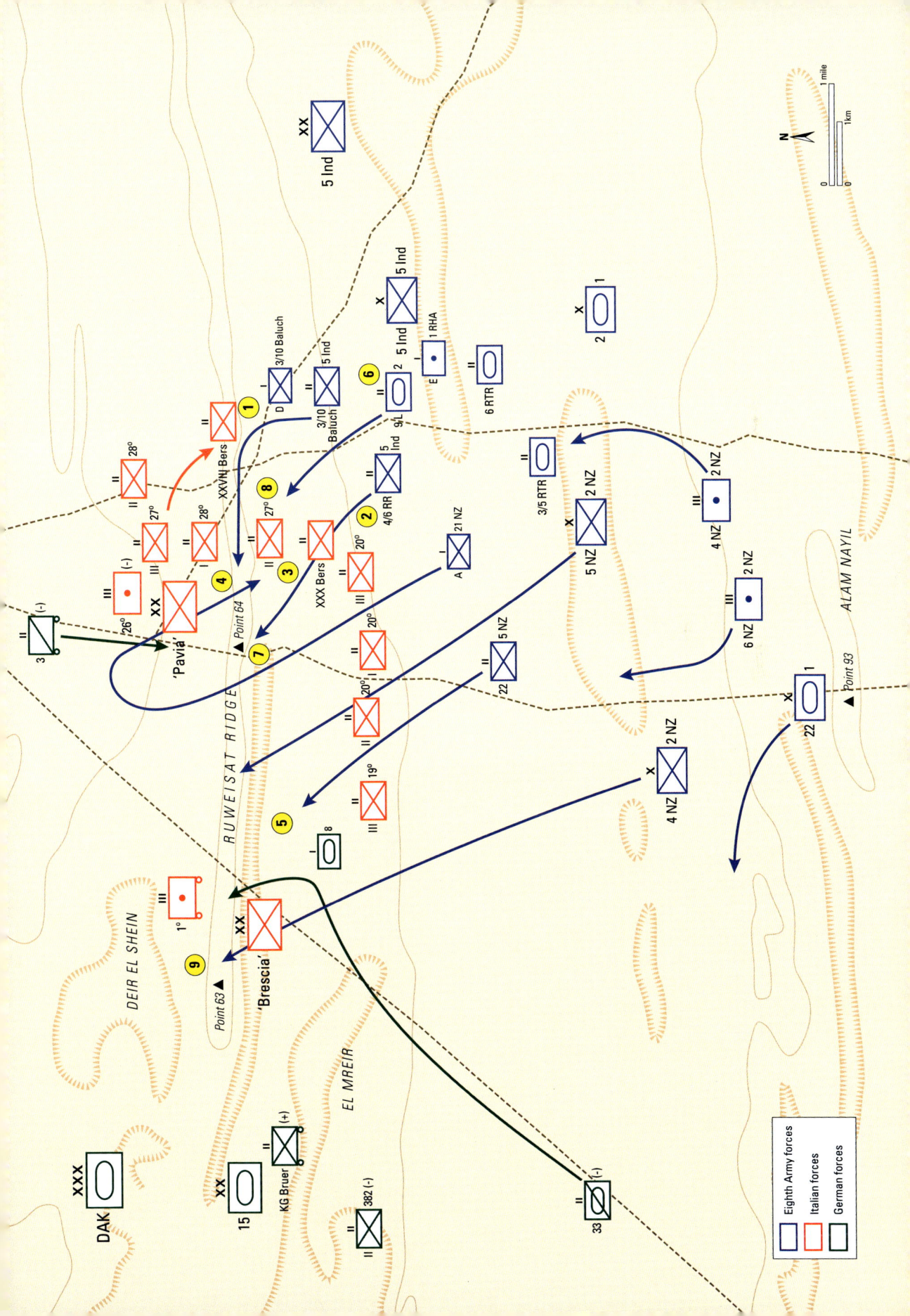

INTO COMBAT

During the action, 3/10 Baluch had Captain Chatterji's C Coy on the right and Lieutenant Sardar Ali's D Coy on the left supported by two platoons of B Coy, with Captain Hamid Khan's A Coy the reserve. Lieutenant-Colonel Taylor's battalion headquarters was located in the centre. To the left was 4/6 Rajputana Rifles. To the Indians' left, 5 NZ Brigade was to march forward 6 miles on a 2.5-mile-wide frontage, also with two battalions up. Each NZ battalion occupied a 1.2-mile frontage, with each company given 0.6 miles if two companies deployed forward. Moving at 1.5 mph, 21 NZ Battalion had to cover 4 miles. Another battalion followed on 1,640yd behind. The battalion's 2-pdr anti-tank guns and the brigade's 6-pdr anti-tank guns brought up the rear. Battalion mortars and the brigade's MMGs accompanied Brigade HQ. The New Zealanders thought the main enemy force occupied entrenchments on the ridge with only an outpost line on the forward slope, but the forward line was the main line. This was in contrast to the Axis positions facing the Indians. Forward enemy positions would be bypassed by the New Zealanders with the battalion in reserve needing to mop up these positions.

The frontage of 5 NZ Brigade was supposed to be 0.6 miles by the time the brigade got to the enemy line. Lieutenant-Colonel Allen, CO 21 NZ Battalion, thought each battalion needed to cover this distance and he spaced his sections at 60yd intervals. In the event, this meant Italian positions were missed. At dawn these positions would stop the machine guns, mortars and guns from reaching the ridge quickly. With Allen soon out of touch partly because of the width of frontage, subordinate commanders would need to use their initiative to continue on to the objective.

At 0000hrs, 3/10 Baluch had the British minefield behind it. The battalion took 40 prisoners by dawn, having attacked the positions of the

Despondent Indian prisoners of the Italian Army, Libya, early 1942. These soldiers lack greatcoats, but appear to have been issued Italian camouflage shelter-halves. (Mondadori via Getty Images)

28° Reggimento di fanteria. On its left, 4/6 Rajputana Rifles was targeted by the II/27° Reggimento di fanteria and guns of the I/26° Reggimento artiglieria, the Indian battalion needing to advance an extra mile to reach the Italian defences. Targeted from an Italian strongpoint and with Axis minefields close by, 4/6 Rajputana Rifles lost cohesion and was pinned down. Some 2.5 miles behind the Indians, 2 Armoured Brigade awaited orders to advance; 22 Armoured Brigade, positioned by Alam Nayil, was also awaiting orders. At dawn, Taylor noticed the plight of 4/6 Rajputana Rifles and ordered D Coy around the minefield. The company obtained a footing on Point 64, but was forced back by mortar fire when Lieutenant Ali was wounded. Later that day, 4/6 Rajputana Rifles moved around and out of the minefield, taking 1,000 prisoners.

The Indian success was in part facilitated by the New Zealanders' movements. A Coy, 21 NZ Battalion plus strays were on the right of 5 NZ Brigade near the Indians. Captain E.B. Butcher, OC A Coy, had Lieutenant K.C. West-Watson's 9 Platoon. His 8 Platoon was missing, though 23 NZ Battalion's 17 Platoon had turned up. Allen met up with them and ordered the advance to continue; by 0245hrs a minefield with fence guarding a gun emplacement was encountered. The noise of multiple lorries was heard. They had mistakenly advanced up to 2 miles beyond the ridge line. Allen departed the group at 0300hrs, ordering them to entrench, to get the other elements of his battalion. He and Staff Sergeant Robert .J. Philip then stumbled on an Italian strongpoint. Allen was shot and died the same day. Philip was bayoneted and shot; at dawn he noticed a lorry driven by NZ soldiers who took the casualties to a first-aid station.

With no sign of Allen, Butcher decided to withdraw at 0345hrs. The group met up with Major H.M. McElroy with elements of HQ Coy and 7 Platoon of A Coy. McElroy was taking his party east off the ridge and had run into a large Italian strongpoint. With ammunition running low, he

A 47/32 modello 35 cannon. Designed by the Austrian Böhler firm, this artillery piece was adopted by the Italian Army in 1935 to provide the infantry with direct-fire support and anti-tank capabilities. Although it lacked a gun shield, the weapon's small size meant concealment from enemy armour could be maintained, especially when it was sited amid rocky terrain. *Bersaglieri* battalions were assigned up to three platoons, each with four guns. Armour-piercing, high-explosive and hollow-charge rounds could be used. (SeM/Universal Images Group via Getty Images)

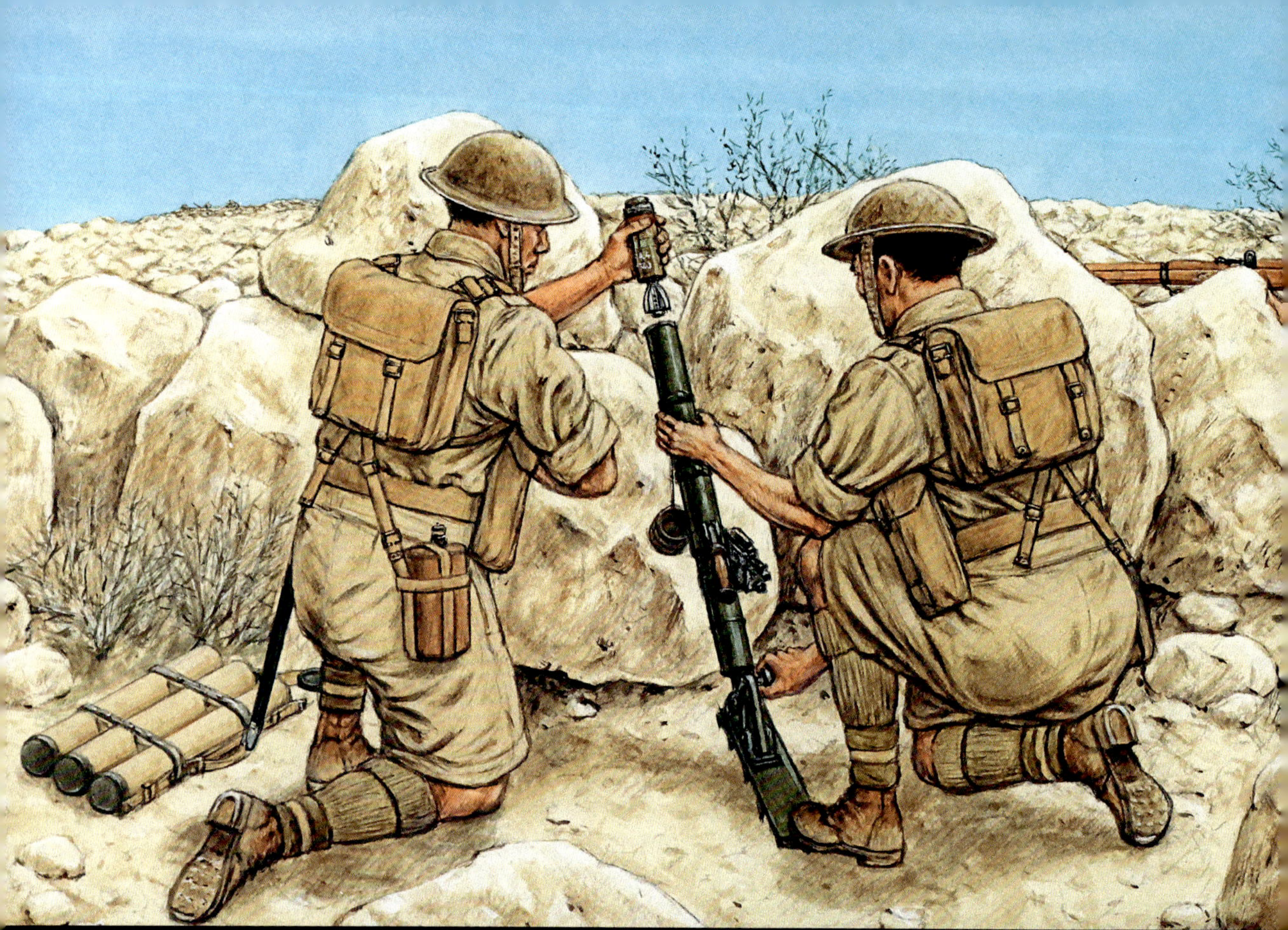

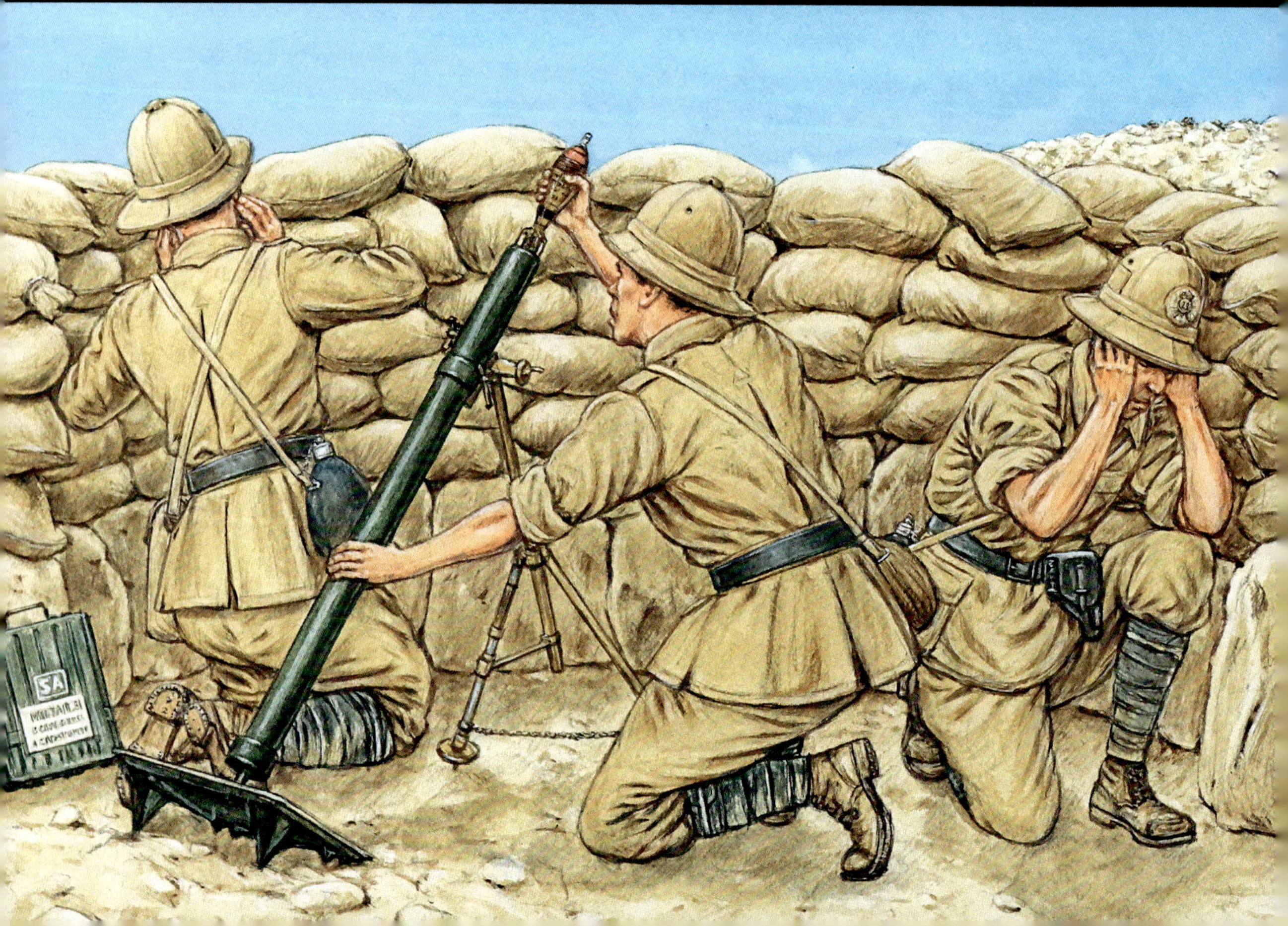
SA

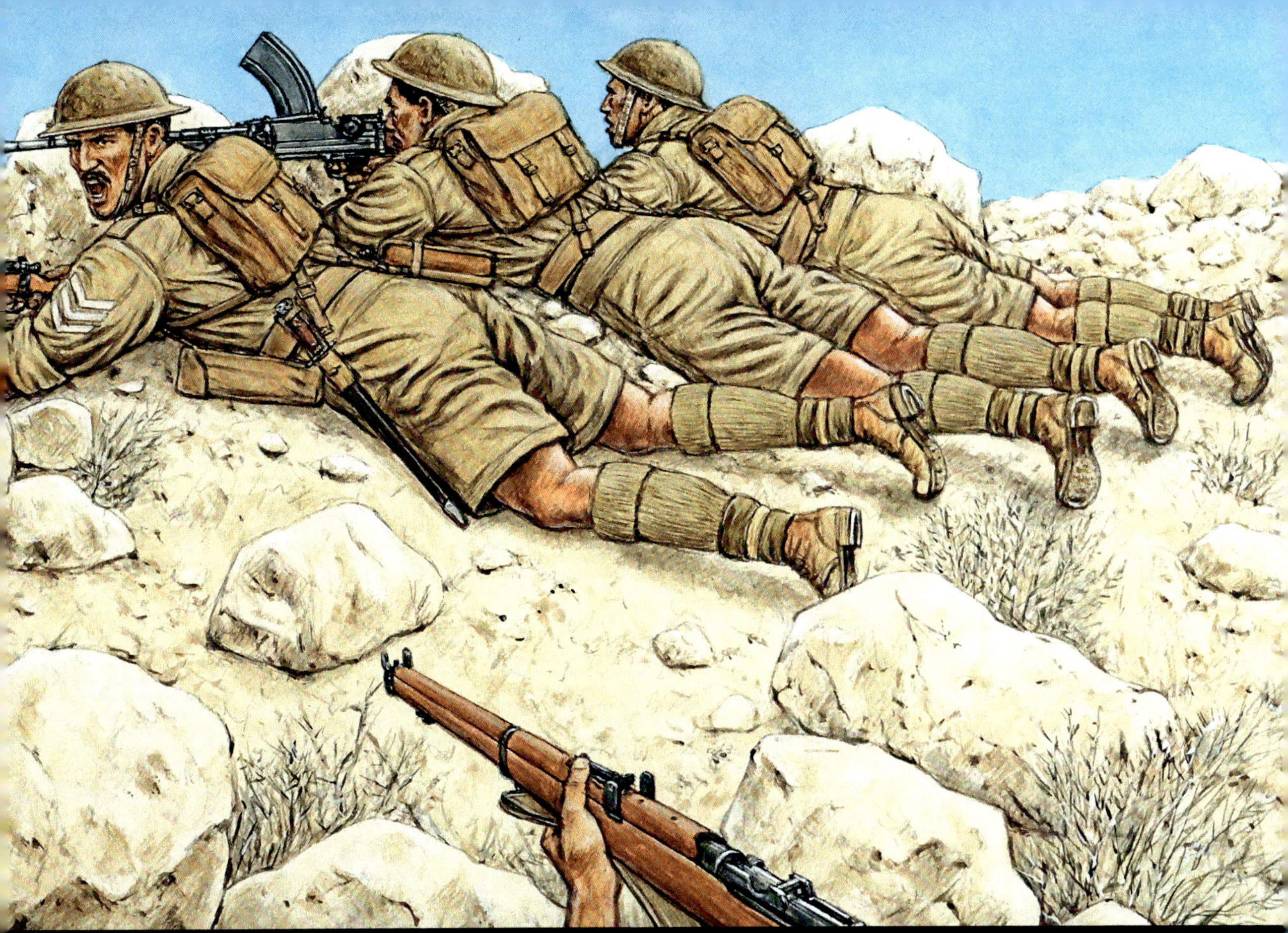

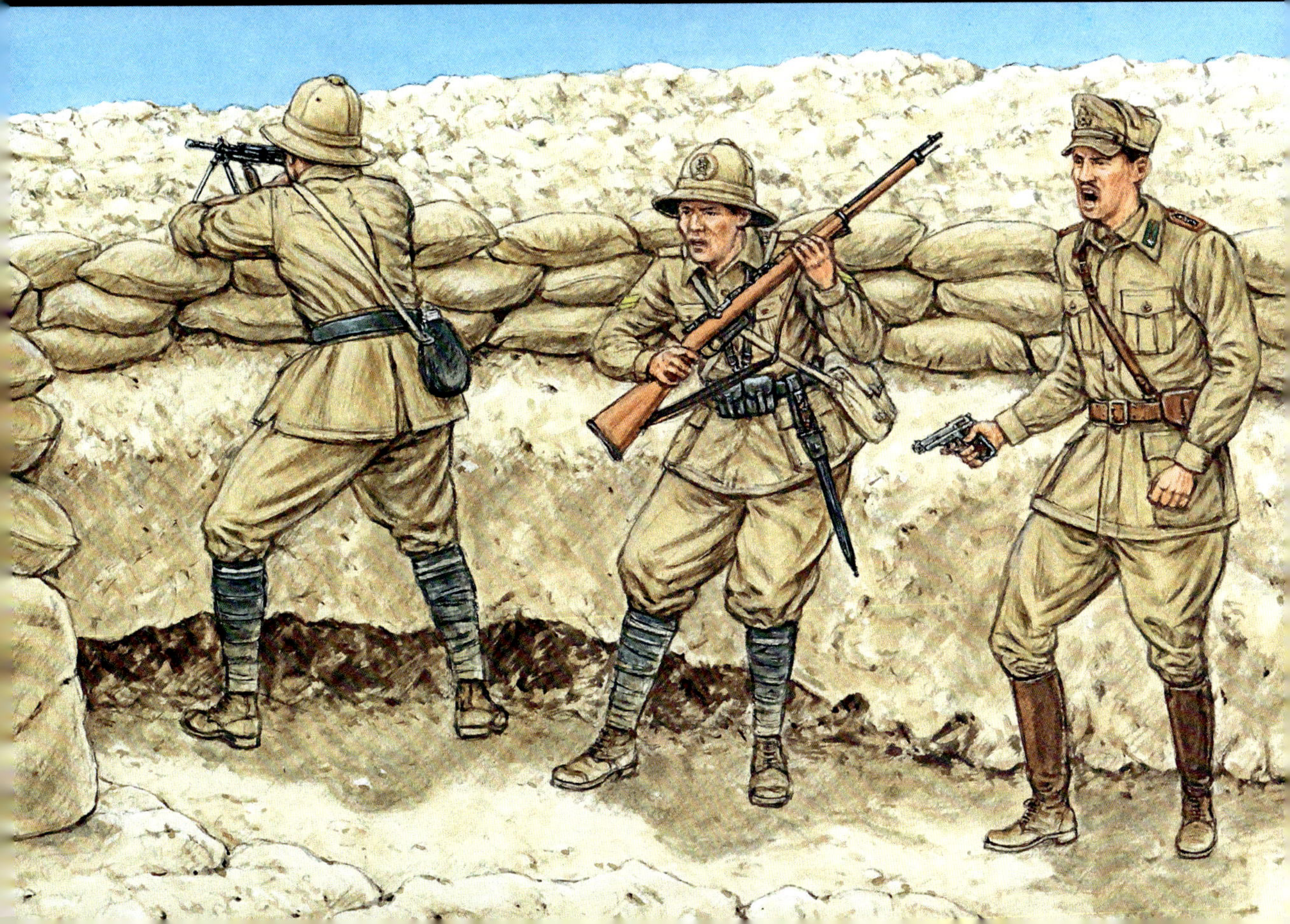

Ruweisat Ridge, 15 July 1942

Indian view: With the coming of dawn, Lieutenant-Colonel Taylor, OC 3/10 Baluch, could see 4/6 Rajputana Rifles held up by heavy Axis fire. He sent his D Coy, commanded by Lieutenant Sardar Ali, towards Point 64 on Ruweisat Ridge to assist. The top was rocky and when the Indians gained the crest of the ridge they commenced moving along it from east to west. They could see Italian mortar and artillery positions to the north of the ridge firing at 4/6 Rajputana Rifles, which had approached the height to the left of 3/10 Baluch. Here, personnel of D Coy target an Italian mortar position with a 2in mortar, covered by a Bren gun.

Italian view: The Axis defence of Ruweisat Ridge was based on entrenching infantry on the southern slope because the terrain near the top was too rocky to build many positions easily. The XXX Battaglione bersaglieri and the II/27° Reggimento di fanteria were holding these positions during the initial stages of the Allied assault and had held up 4/6 Rajputana Rifles. On the northern slope, shown here, the I/28° Reggimento di fanteria was supported by gun positions of the 26° Reggimento artiglieria. An 81/14 modello 35 mortar can be seen firing rounds at Allied positions on the southern slope. An observer, formerly stationed on the crest, has had to return hastily with the Baluchis' approach. The officer, his shoulder boards denoting the 28° Reggimento di fanteria, has spotted the Indians and ordered an infantryman with a Breda 30 LMG to target them.

ordered a bayonet charge and succeeded in taking the position along with several hundred prisoners, probably from the XXX Battaglione bersaglieri. This NZ group of seven officers and 60 men had 500 Italian prisoners, mostly men from 'Pavia'. Captain C.G. Ironside was killed and eight men were wounded from the group. Casualties to 5 NZ Brigade were light, only 35 killed, wounded or missing to 21 NZ Battalion. The 6-pdr anti-tank guns did not get to the ridge, however, because of the suspected presence of Axis armour.

With the next day yet to dawn, 5 NZ Brigade was in the central part of the ridge and 4 NZ Brigade was on Point 63 to the left. Generale di brigata Giacomo Lombardi, the commander of 'Brescia', was captured but managed to free himself. Most positions of 'Brescia' had been bypassed by the attackers, and needed to be neutralized on the forward slope. Both 23 NZ Battalion and 21 NZ Battalion encountered German tanks and destroyed at least three of them; 22 NZ Battalion mopped up many positions and Brigadier Kippenberger ordered the battalion to entrench on the southern slope with K Troop, 33 Anti-Tank Battery, Royal New Zealand Artillery (RNZA). Kippenberger did not have good communication links with his battalions because their No. 18 radio sets had poor range and limited battery life. The laying of cables did not proceed smoothly, meaning no telephone connection was established. Supported by three troops of 6-pdrs and two platoons of MMGs, 4 NZ Brigade was established on the ridge 1 mile west of 5 NZ Brigade. When 6 Field Regiment RNZA commenced the approach to the ridge, the gunners were targeted and the trucks took cover in a wadi where they stayed at first light. The artillery observers had accompanied the infantry and could not be contacted.

At dawn, 5 Indian Brigade was held up by 'Pavia'. At the time of the attack, the III/27° Reggimento di fanteria was occupying the positions of the XXVIII Battaglione bersaglieri and was caught when deploying with heavy weapons still on lorries and had only two companies left. The

Indian Army personnel examine an Axis 8.8cm gun captured during the fight for Sidi Omar, Libya, 22 December 1941. These formidable weapons were used by German and Italian crews against both aerial and ground targets throughout the Desert War. During the battle for Ruweisat Ridge, the British tankers might have thought the German armoured cars were in the business of luring them into range of 8.8cm anti-tank guns. Tank support was provided, but this was not close support. The lack of orders should not have stopped the tank commanders from seeing the urgency of the situation and responding. Had the British tanks moved up earlier, the Italian positions bypassed in the early-morning advance might have surrendered quickly. The few tanks the Germans had south of the slope had probably departed. The British tanks when they did get going only moved into the Indian sector. (Bettmann/Getty Images)

II/27° Reggimento di fanteria was isolated, though still holding its position. The 28° Reggimento di fanteria's positions had also held and had not been surrounded. Though closest to the Indian formations, the XXX Battaglione bersaglieri was routed partly because NZ elements had strayed behind the positions it occupied. By 1000hrs, the II/27° Reggimento di fanteria and the I/26° Reggimento artiglieria were finished. Later in the morning, the remaining companies of the III/27° Reggimento di fanteria withdrew to the I/28° Reggimento di fanteria, forming a defensive flank to the south.

At dawn, 22 NZ Battalion on the southern slope noticed armour from the west and south envelop the position they occupied. About 8–10 tanks in two groups could be seen in the half-light. Expecting British support, the New Zealanders had a rude awakening when machine guns opened up on them. Taken by surprise, the four 6-pdr crews managed to destroy two of the tanks and damaged others. The other tanks put the NZ guns out of action, though. A total of 14 officers and 261 men from 22 NZ Battalion surrendered. Kippenberger had only just departed and the carrier in which he was travelling was fired upon. Kippenberger got back to Major-General L.M. Inglis, acting GOC 2nd NZ Division, and told him the brigade was being attacked by tanks. He dashed off to 2 Armoured Brigade, found Major-General Lumsden and explained the situation. Lumsden reprimanded Brigadier Briggs, OC 2 Armoured Brigade, for failing to be on the ridge by first light. Lumsden's written orders had not specified a time and place, however.

Having been told by Inglis that the attack was faltering, Lumsden ordered 2 Armoured Brigade to advance; but the tanks approached the Indian and not the NZ positions. At 0635hrs, 2 Armoured Brigade got going with 3/5 RTR on the right, 9 Lancers in the centre and 6 RTR on the left. Only one regiment managed to reach the Indians, however: 9 Lancers, accompanied by 25-pdrs of E Battery, 1 RHA. At 1000hrs, 9 Lancers encountered the first Axis strongpoint and fired upon it. By 1400hrs, contact was made with 5 Indian Brigade to help 4/6 Rajputana Rifles, which had not penetrated the Axis defences. By this time, British tanks had reached 5 NZ Brigade opposite a strongpoint and the enemy, under bombardment from 6 Field Regiment RNZA, quickly surrendered. By 1430hrs, with 2 Armoured Brigade tanks in support, the Indians had made contact with the New Zealanders on the ridge and taken Point 64. This meant a route for support weapons to those on the ridge further west was possible. Kippenberger ordered anti-tank guns, carriers, ammunition and mortars up this way. Inglis had thought 1st Armoured Division was following behind his infantry, but no coordinating effort was being made by Gott.

The Deutsches Afrikakorps commander, Generalleutnant Walther Nehring, had at first not thought to counter-attack. Then German armour attacking 22 NZ Battalion had reported enemy anti-tank guns on the ridge and when at 0655hrs the 15. Panzer-Division reported an Allied battalion with anti-tank guns in Deir el Shein, this was too much for Nehring. At 0707hrs, the 21. Panzer-Division was ordered to organize a force for a deployment south-east and by 0840hrs the division's Aufklärungs-Abteilung (mot.) 3 was 2 miles west of Point 63. The battalion commander, Hauptmann Hellmuth Schroetter, could see 3/10 Baluch and by early afternoon the tanks of 2 Armoured Brigade. Nehring also ordered an infantry *Kampfgruppe* from the 15. Panzer-Division and Panzer-Aufklärungs-Abteilung 33 north. The order reached Panzer-

Italian soldiers with a Breda 20/65 mod. 35 anti-aircraft gun under fire at El Alamein, 1942. Armoured cars moving quickly threw up a lot of sand and dust, limiting lines of sight for the anti-tank gunners. Most of the New Zealanders' anti-tank guns were mounted on lorries, which made them easier targets. (Scherl/Süddeutsche Zeitung Photo/Alamy Stock Photo)

Aufklärungs-Abteilung 33 at 0940hrs. Elements of 22 Armoured Brigade forced the infantry *Kampfgruppe* to take a circuitous route to get to 15. Panzer-Division headquarters. Kampfgruppe Bruer, led by Oberst Alfred Bruer and composed of 100 infantry, six machine guns and six light anti-tank guns from the 21. Panzer-Division, also took part; and an understrength company from Panzerjäger-Abteilung 39 joined in.

At 1730hrs, Hauptmann Detlef Lienau, CO Panzer-Aufklärungs-Abteilung 33, reported Point 63 taken; the Indians were the next target. At 1840hrs, Nehring signalled Lienau to march along the top of the ridge and surround the enemy north of Ruweisat Ridge. He was to be supported by Kampfgruppe Bruer on Point 64 and the 15. Panzer-Division infantry group to the south. Bruer, though, was being attacked by tanks and the German infantry group had stopped at the 15. Panzer-Division headquarters. The German counter-attack still managed to destroy most of 4 NZ Brigade and elements of 5 NZ Brigade. Positioned near Indian positions on Point 64, 5 NZ Brigade was ordered to withdraw in the dark.

At 0530hrs on 16 July, the Germans launched the assault on the ridge with elements of the 21. Panzer-Division facing 5 Indian Brigade. Entrenched anti-tank guns and field artillery called in stymied the German tanks. Also on the ridge were elements of 2 Armoured Brigade, with 9 Lancers claiming seven tanks destroyed for no loss. Nehring organized for another attempt at 1925hrs; but he lost elements north when Rommel ordered him to send them to counter the Australians. The British through signals intercepts knew another German assault was impending. Allied artillery targeted German tanks on the southern slopes. On 17 July, German infantry and tank crews awoke to find they were in front of Indian positions. Field guns and anti-tank guns engaged them and they made their way into Deir el Shein. III./PzGrenRgt 104 held its position at Point 63 on the ridge, however.

NZ losses amounted to 1,405 killed, wounded and missing, while the Italians had lost some 2,000 men taken prisoner. Casualties for 3/10 Baluch amounted to only four dead and 16 wounded, including Lieutenant Sardar, Subedar Sultan Khan and Jemadar Dham Pal. When the battalion departed 4th Indian Division during February 1943, Major-General Tuker highlighted the Ruweisat Ridge engagement, saying it was a feat of arms ever to be remembered (Maxwell 2009: 123).

Makh Khad Ridge

17 July 1942

BACKGROUND TO BATTLE

On 5 July 1942, 9th Australian Division elements reached the front line. The 'Sabratha' Infantry Division with three battalions was by the El Alamein box, with the 'Trento' Motorized Division (61° and 62° Reggimenti fanteria motorizzato, each with three battalions) and the 7° Reggimento bersaglieri. Behind these positions stood the 'Trieste' Motorized Division. D Coy, 2/43 Battalion, mounted a raid on Axis anti-tank positions on a nearby ridge on the night of 7/8 July. The raiders destroyed four anti-tank guns and blew up several immobilized M3 Stuart light tanks nearby.

On 8 July, Major-General Ramsden, GOC XXX Corps, ordered the Australians to assault Tel el Eisa by the coast road and the South Africans to target Makh Khad; 26 Australian Brigade was chosen to lead. Supported by 44 RTR and 9th Divisional Cavalry, 2/24 and 2/48 battalions stood by. Each Australian infantry battalion had machine guns, anti-tank guns, engineers and tanks assigned. The advance was a success: the II/86° Reggimento di fanteria was smashed and the II/85° Reggimento di fanteria and the X/7° Reggimento bersaglieri were isolated. Although the headquarters of the 7° Reggimento bersaglieri was overrun, 2 South African Brigade was halted at Makh Khad when its supporting tanks were knocked out. The I/85° Reggimento di fanteria was brought up from Bardia. 'Trieste' deployed the II/66° Reggimento fanteria motorizzato. A German battalion from Infanterie-Regiment 382 also arrived.

On 11 July, 'Trento' threw back another South African attempt to take Miteiriya Ridge. The Australians did the damage with two battalions of 'Sabratha' and three artillery groups destroyed; 350 men from the 7° Reggimento bersaglieri and the II/66° Reggimento fanteria motorizzato were also lost. Rommel cited morale issues with the Italians (Montanari 2007: 135). Serious deficiencies in cohesion and a shortage of good officers led to the poor performance by 'Sabratha', though the I/85° Reggimento di fanteria was seen to be an exception.

On 12 July, an Axis counter-attack conducted against 26 Australian Brigade by the X/7° Reggimento bersaglieri on the coast, II./IR 382 in the centre and the I/85° Reggimento di fanteria on the right gained half a mile. Rommel planned to attack with his armour on 13 July, a fact known to the British through intercepts. The Axis attempt on the El Alamein box failed, as did another attack on the Australian salient on 14 July, supported by the I/66° Reggimento fanteria motorizzato.

On 16 July the Australians attacked Tel el Eisa with 2/23 Battalion supported by elements of 8 RTR and 44 RTR. Stationed on Point 25 with 200 men, the I/85° Reggimento di fanteria soon collapsed. The Australians then attacked part of I./IR 382 and the I/86° Reggimento di fanteria, defeating them also. A counter-attack by III./IR 382 halted the Australians; then the III/39° Reggimento di fanteria and later a

Australian troops at Tobruk, 21 October 1941. During the siege of Tobruk, 2/43 Battalion's experiences – 191 days in total, 124 on the front line – made the men battle-hardened. The worst time was during July 1941, when the battalion deployed to the 'Salient', where the Germans had captured nearby fortifications and the enemy was close by. During 16–18 July, 80 poorly trained new soldiers arrived and soon received a baptism of fire. On 3 August, B Coy, which had incorporated 40 new replacements, was tasked with making a night raid on the enemy lines. Despite an abundance of supporting fire from 16 MMGs and 70 guns and mortars, the company could not take the heavily fortified Axis positions, suffering 102 casualties; only 30 soldiers returned unscathed. (Bettmann/Getty Images)

battalion from Panzergrenadier-Regiment 104 got to the line. The commander of 'Sabratha' did not commit the III/39° Reggimento di fanteria because it was composed of men with little knowledge of weapons and lacked training.

The next punch was delivered on 17 July by 24 Australian Brigade, further south-east. To divert the Germans further from Ruweisat Ridge, the British ordered the Australians to attack Makh Khad and then Miteiriya Ridge. During the initial attack, 24 Australian Brigade would deploy 2/32 Battalion to capture Makh Khad; then 2/43 Battalion, supported by elements of 44 RTR and 9th Divisional Cavalry, would push on through and seize Miteiriya Ridge. The first objective was to be taken by 0300hrs, with 2/43 Battalion due to begin its advance at 0520hrs. The 65° Reggimento fanteria motorizzato occupied positions mostly on 2/32 Battalion's route of advance, with the II/66° Reggimento fanteria motorizzato on its left; the 62° Reggimento fanteria motorizzato stood opposite 2/43 Battalion. The II/61° Reggimento fanteria motorizzato would be brought up to the front and take position during the day.

Ordered to seize Makh Khad Ridge from Trig 22 to the Qattara Track, 2/32 Battalion departed by lorry from the El Alamein box at 2050hrs on 16 July. D Coy was to push along the telephone line to the junction with the Qattara Track, with the other companies following once the junction was captured. Forming-up positions would then place A Coy forward on the right 2,000yd west of the Qattara Track, B Coy on a ridge 1,000yd west of the Qattara Track and C Coy on the Qattara Track with a platoon further east; artillery observers would accompany them, with two artillery batteries on call. The assault was to commence from these positions at 0230hrs on 17 July. D Coy reported by radio that it had reached the junction at 0100hrs with no enemy encountered. By 0200hrs the other companies had passed through. The battalion's tactical headquarters then marched to the junction, with D Coy going into reserve.

MAP KEY

1 **0230hrs:** A Coy, B Coy and C Coy, 2/32 Battalion, pass through D Coy and the Australian assault towards Makh Khad Ridge commences.

2 **0250–0515hrs:** A Coy, 2/32 Battalion, bypasses Point 22 and ascends a height 1,500yd further on. The isolated Australian company is exposed.

3 **0525–0730hrs:** B Coy, 9th Divisional Cavalry, with seven Crusader tanks and four infantry carrier platoons, commences a forward approach at 0525hrs. Two Crusaders are hit by Italian anti-tank guns, probably from the II/65° Reggimento fanteria motorizzato. Mechanical faults force a third Crusader out of the battle.

4 **0600–0730hrs:** 2/43 Battalion begins its assault on Miteiriya Ridge at 0600hrs, with B Coy reaching the ridge at 0703hrs. At 0730hrs, C Coy elements assault positions occupied by the I and III/46° Reggimento artiglieria, destroying three Italian guns and taking 150 prisoners. D Coy occupies positions 500yd south-west of the ridge.

5 **0700–0730hrs:** Axis forces recapture Point 22 on Makh Khad Ridge. Less one platoon, D Coy, 2/32 Battalion attempts to take it back, but the Australians' success is only temporary, with MMG and mortar fire driving 17 Platoon off.

6 **0750hrs:** With the supporting armour squadron now down to six tanks, 2/43 Battalion commences a withdrawal from Miteiriya Ridge.

7 **1000hrs:** German armoured cars and tanks attack positions occupied by B Coy and C Coy, 2/32 Battalion; three Axis tanks and two armoured cars are immobilized.

8 **1200–1400hrs:** Following a further Axis assault with AFVs supported by infantry, a platoon of B Coy, 2/32 Battalion withdraws. By 1400hrs Captain Joshua, OC B Coy, has regained control.

9 **1700–1730hrs:** Two platoons of C Coy, 2/32 Battalion, are overrun by an Axis assault involving the II/61° Reggimento fanteria motorizzato. With Point 22 also occupied by Axis forces, 2/32 Battalion's position is difficult and it is ordered to withdraw.

10 **1830hrs:** By this time, 2/43 Battalion occupies positions along the line of departure; 2/28 Battalion begins to advance to positions along the Qattara Track by the telephone line.

Battlefield environment

North of the railway line and near the coast, a low ridge ran from Trig 26 to Trig 33; this area was seized by 26 Australian Brigade on 9 July when it conducted an assault from the El Alamein box. From Trig 33 the Australians turned south towards the low rise bisected by the railway line; here Tel el Eisa was the highest point. The Australians held off German and Italian counter-attacks through to 16 July. Makh Khad Ridge was 2 miles south of this point and on the other side of the telephone line, which ran roughly parallel and south of the railway line. Not a particularly long feature, Makh Khad Ridge ran south-east about 2.5 miles from the railway line. Trig 22, situated on a spur jutting out from the ridge, was the highest point. The terrain was stony on the ridge itself, with scrub and softer ground to the north-east and south-west.

Running south-west from the railway line, the Qattara Track reached a point 1 mile south-east of Trig 22 and then ran south-south-west to Trig 30 on Miteiriya Ridge, some 3.7 miles away. Running parallel to the railway line, the ridge permitted good observation of the El Alamein box, about 5 miles distant; Italian artillery was concealed behind the slope. The ground to the south-west of Miteiriya Ridge was composed of a succession of dips and rises, the highest elevation being 154ft. Abundant scrub gave the Italians some concealment by the track and Trigs 30 and 33. Miteiriya Ridge featured stony ground in which it was difficult to build entrenchments.

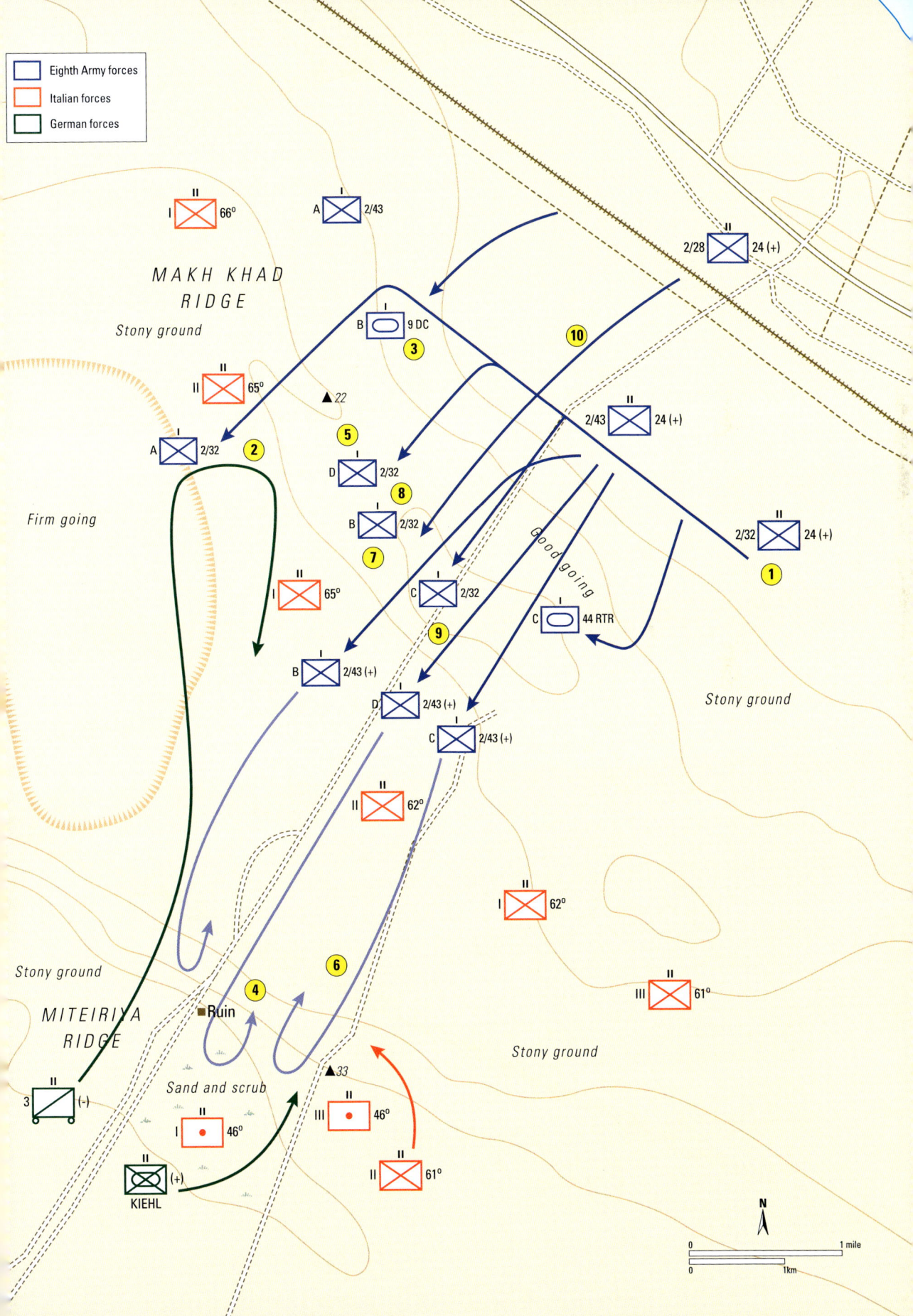

Eighth Army forces
Italian forces
German forces

MAKH KHAD
RIDGE

Stony ground

I ☒ 66°
A ☒ 2/43
II ☒ 2/28 24 (+)

B ▭ 9 DC
③

II ☒ 65°
▲ 22

⑤

A ☒ 2/32 ②
D ☒ 2/32
⑧
B ☒ 2/32
⑦

Firm going

I ☒ 65°

C ☒ 2/32
⑨

C ▭ 44 RTR

Good going

Stony ground

2/43 ☒ 24 (+)

2/32 ☒ 24 (+) ①

B ☒ 2/43 (+)
D ☒ 2/43 (+)
C ☒ 2/43 (+)

II ☒ 62°

I ☒ 62°

III ☒ 61°

Stony ground

MITEIRIYA
RIDGE

⑥

④

■ Ruin

▲ 33

Sand and scrub

3 ◱ (-)

I ⊡ 46°
III ⊡ 46°

KIEHL ☒ (+)

II ☒ 61°

Stony ground

N

0   1 mile
0   1km

INTO COMBAT

At 0230hrs the assault began. A Coy, 2/43 Battalion, with a troop of 6-pdrs under command, was ordered to cover the right flank and maintain contact with 26 Australian Brigade elements deployed further north-west.

A Coy, 2/32 Battalion, marched towards Point 22, an important height for enemy observation and heavily defended. At 0250hrs a firefight commenced. By 0330hrs the Australians took the height, though the battalion radio was not working properly and messages could only be heard from A Coy. At 0515hrs, A Coy reported that it had overshot the objective and might withdraw some distance. At 0530hrs a machine-gun platoon, two anti-tank troops and two mortar detachments supporting the battalion moved through on lorries to Point 22, though they soon had to dismount and take cover on the reverse slope. Lieutenant R.W. Cameron's machine-gun platoon from 2/2 Machine Gun Battalion marched on foot and Cameron contacted Captain K.B. Forwood, OC A Coy, who was now 1,500yd from Point 22. Forwood was too far forward – on the main ridge, rather than on the spur upon which Point 22 was situated – and Cameron suggested shifting back to Point 22, where Cameron had left his guns. Forwood, who had taken 50 Italians prisoner, wanted Cameron to cover his right flank from the north-west. Heavy Axis fire from the west and north-west stopped Cameron getting back to his platoon for 2½ hours.

B Coy had no trouble seizing the position assigned to it and took 60 prisoners. C Coy got to the Qattara Track and at first light, Captain P.R. Jacoby, OC C Coy, positioned a platoon to the east of the track; C Coy had taken 50 prisoners. At 0530hrs, D Coy was sent forward of the junction and 1,000yd west of the track where the company could dig entrenchments. At this time, 2/32 Battalion occupied some 2,500yd of line and its companies were separated. The main activity was at Point 22 and to the south-west. A Coy was last seen by members of B Coy at 0630hrs. Lieutenant J.N. Liddell, with some of his platoon, would make his way out later.

At 0600hrs the enemy opened up with MMGs and guns on B Coy. C Coy had six Axis tanks or armoured cars approach them, pinning down the whole company. These probably belonged to Kampfgruppe Kiehl; this formation included a company of captured M3 Stuart tanks. The Australians rejected a surrender demand and stayed for two hours because the anti-tank guns accompanying C Coy could not target them. A captured Italian 20/65 gun was used by 13 Platoon to knock out three of the Axis vehicles. The platoon from 2/2 Machine Gun Battalion got their machine guns into position and provided fire support.

The crest of Miteiriya Ridge was swept with fire by the Italians; by 0700hrs the Australians had lost the ridge and D Coy, less one platoon, was ordered to take it again. Axis machine guns targeted D Coy. Lieutenant M.J. O'Mara's 17 Platoon got to Point 22, though they had to withdraw behind the crest. Axis mortars and guns targeted O'Mara's men from high ground to the west and 16 Platoon lost its commander, prompting the platoon to withdraw. The assault failed, though some 50 men were rallied north of the telegraph line.

By 0900hrs, Axis artillery bombardments of the area of operations commenced. At about 1000hrs, Axis tanks and armoured cars, which had

An Australian soldier 're-christens' El Alamein railway station, August 1942. (Mirrorpix/Mirrorpix via Getty Images)

Australian soldiers fraternize with British troops wearing non-standard webbing gear, El Alamein, 12 July 1942. The triangular hat insignia suggests the Australians are members of either 2/3 Machine-Gun Battalion or 2/3 Pioneer Battalion. (Fix/Imperial War Museums via Getty Images)

hitherto maintained a continuous fire on Point 22 without attempting to move up the slope, moved under cover of the escarpment to where B Coy and C Coy were situated. Australian anti-tank guns immobilized three tanks and two armoured cars; the others withdrew. A further approach by them was made at 1200hrs. A 2-pdr had to be moved forward to target the Axis vehicles, and Australian gunners were hit. One platoon from B Coy withdrew as the Axis tanks maintained position, firing at the platoon. This was witnessed by other platoons, which also sought to get back. By 1400hrs, Captain R. Joshua, OC B Coy, was able to prevent them from withdrawing.

At 1700hrs, the Axis forces made a further approach at the juncture of C Coy and 2/43 Battalion. The two forward platoons of C Coy were overrun and the remainder withdrew through B Coy. Axis troops were on Point 22 and D Coy sent up a platoon to attempt to throw them back, but the platoon could not dislodge the enemy. At 1730hrs, 2/32 Battalion got permission from brigade to form a line covering the track along the telephone line to the Qattara Track to join up with 2/43 Battalion. C Coy had lost its commander, Captain Jacoby, wounded at 1600hrs and had only a single officer; the company was placed on the left. A platoon of B Coy was left on Point 22 owing to many of its personnel having been wounded and was only pulled out at 2400hrs.

A Coy, 2/32 Battalion, had lost the most men: Captain Forwood, Lieutenant L.O. Neumann and Lieutenant R.M. Willington were taken prisoner along with 34 enlisted men. B Coy lost eight men killed, 26 wounded and 12 taken prisoner. D Coy lost four men killed, 14 wounded and 28 taken

Born in 1919 to Methodist parents, Allan Jones was a motor painter from Renmark, 160 miles north-east of Adelaide, South Australia. He was slight, 5ft 7in, and joined the militia aged 17. Attending the militia camp during June 1940 and hearing France was lost, he asked for permission to go to Adelaide to enlist for overseas service. He joined 18 Platoon, D Coy, 2/43 Battalion.

During the passage to North Africa, Jones was made a lance corporal of 7 Section; during the siege of Tobruk he complained about his platoon officer, Lieutenant Grant, to the company commander, Captain Jeanes. Jones wanted to be demoted and lost his rank. A brigade inquiry led to Grant being moved to the battalion quartermaster position, though he soon returned to D Coy as OC 16 Platoon; Grant was subsequently OC D Coy. Jones was trained on the 2in mortar when the weapon was issued in early 1942 and was attached to platoon headquarters. He served in 2/43 Battalion through to October 1942, by which time he was an acting corporal, and had his rank confirmed after Second El Alamein.

Jones was a section leader when the battalion received jungle training at Cairns, Queensland, during June 1943. He deployed to New Guinea and by October was acting platoon commander when his sergeant was wounded. Landing with 706 men in September 1943, 2/43 Battalion sustained 758 casualties by January 1944, 600 to disease and 158 to the enemy, though 180 replacements had arrived. During July 1944, Jones trained with the battalion at Cairns, but was then posted to the Jungle Warfare Training Centre at Canungra, Queensland, to be an instructor. By April 1945, Jones was with a training battalion at Bonegilla, Victoria. After being demobilized he worked as a motor refurbisher and polisher. Allan Jones died in February 2001.

---

prisoner and C Coy two men killed, 18 wounded and 24 taken prisoner. Brigade listed the battalion as having lost 24 killed, seven officers and 73 men wounded, and three officers and 137 men missing. These losses meant only 285 men could be formed for further operations.

Ordered to assist with the assault of Point 22, 9th Divisional Cavalry provided west-flank protection. Operating with the Australian cavalry were C Sqn, 44 RTR; a troop of 6-pdr anti-tank guns; a troop of 25-pdr field guns; and five Stuart light tanks. Captain H.G. Fyffe, OC B Sqn, had two troops of Crusader tanks and four carrier troops, plus a headquarters troop with one Crusader and four carriers. Lieutenants I. Crompton and P. Kelly commanded the Crusader troops. C Sqn, 44 RTR, was to assist the initial assault if needed, and then help with the advance on Miteiriya Ridge.

Ordered to follow and provide right-flank support, Fyffe's B Sqn commenced a forward advance by 0525hrs, with the carriers of 10 Troop ordered to get to a point for forward observation. Light shelling began, though no Australian vehicles were hit. The artillery observer halted after 700yd to bring fire to bear on the Axis guns. Fyffe's Crusader halted after 1,000yd on a low ridge. On Fyffe's left, 10 Troop was hull down with a Crusader from 7 Troop a few hundred yards ahead of him. The squadron was behind while Fyffe took a look at the enemy situation. Crompton ahead had encountered an Italian anti-tank gun at close range, concealed in scrub. He took his tank behind the low ridge with Fyffe and was not targeted. His other two Crusaders did not accompany him because they mistook the SHQ Crusader for Fyffe's and stayed with this tank. Fyffe ordered a platoon of Crusaders around the right to outflank the enemy on the low ridge to the front. Concealed anti-tank guns targeted the Crusaders and one was knocked out.

Then SHQ received information that enemy tanks had used a smokescreen to advance on the Australians' right flank. Less one tank that had broken

Gherardo Vaiarini

Born in 1891, Gherardo Vaiarini grew up in Concusio, Brescia, a province of Lombardy. He attended the Modena Military Academy, graduating in 1913. Joining the 77º Reggimento di fanteria as a *sottotenente*, Vaiarini fought at the battle of Gorizia (6–17 August 1916), during the most successful Italian offensive on the Isonzo River. He was seriously wounded in 1917, but did resume military service with the Aegean Occupation forces. During 1924–27 he was at the Brescia Military District and upon promotion to *maggiore* was with the Military Command at Udine. By 1935 he was a *tenente colonnello* and commander of the 77º Reggimento di fanteria. When Vaiarini was made a *colonello* he was the commander of the 65º Reggimento fanteria motorizzato; he took his regiment to the Alps to fight the French during June 1940, having been made a *Cavaliere Ordine Militaire d'Italia* on 1 June.

Departing with his regiment for North Africa in August 1941, Vaiarini led his regiment during the battle for Makh Khad on 17 July 1942. During the Makh Khad battle he was with the II/65º Reggimento fanteria motorizzato and was probably caught out by the assault conducted by A Coy, 2/32 Battalion. Though this Australian company was exposed because it had overshot its objective by 1,500yd, the Italians bypassed by the Australians were also isolated, with MMGs firing at them when the day dawned. The attempts to extricate the Italians and make A Coy prisoners led to some ferocious fighting, during which Vaiarini was wounded. He died the same day when being transported to the field hospital at El Daba. Prior to his death, he wrote: 'Long live the 65th. It does not matter if I die. Long live Italy.' Vaiarini was awarded the *Medaglia d'Oro al Valor Militare*.

down, 8 Troop was sent to take a look. Soon after, 8 Troop reported that a Crusader was lost when the troop ran into some anti-tank guns. This was Kelly's tank, hit by a shell that entered the turret and detonated some grenades stored inside it. Fyffe ordered the Crusader with engine trouble to be towed off the battlefield. Now he had only one troop of Crusaders left. At 1000hrs the artillery observer's tank, a Stuart, was located with squadron headquarters. Friendly infantry positions could not be determined with accuracy, though the Italians could be seen hauling two anti-tank guns to positions on the low ridge. The artillery observer brought down fire on them and their crews dispersed.

Fyffe was ordered to go forward, but he thought this was not possible. He did not comply with an order to push on around the left flank with carriers. At 1300hrs Fyffe's four Crusaders probed forward again 300yd on the right flank. Brigade informed him to be careful about firing forward as friendly infantry could be nearby. At 1400hrs, friendly artillery mistakenly targeted the Australian tanks and B Sqn was immediately sent 1 mile back. During the late afternoon, artillery shells landed in the area in which the tanks had harboured, this time causing some Australian casualties. On the morning of 18 July the squadron would manage to join up with A Coy, 2/43 Battalion, the company with which it was supposed to be operating on 17 July. Two further Crusaders would depart the squadron because of issues, leaving Fyffe with two Crusaders and the carriers.

The soldiers of 2/43 Battalion had no sleep late on 16 July. Lorries transported them from the El Alamein box on the road between the coast and the railway line and then through sand for 1 mile south of the road. The assault from Makh Khad to Miteiriya Ridge would be conducted in daylight. Despite having received no indication of 2/32 Battalion's success or otherwise, Lieutenant-Colonel W.J. Wain, CO 2/43 Battalion, decided to press on. At 0525hrs, 2/43 Battalion debussed near the track's junction with the telegraph

An Italian gun crew haul their 47/32 anti-tank gun. (DE AGOSTINI PICTURE LIBRARY/Getty Images)

line and passed through 2/32 Battalion at 0600hrs, 40 minutes late and in full daylight. B Coy was forward on the right of the track, C Coy was on the left and D Coy was on each side of the track, 500yd back; battalion headquarters was with D Coy's rear element and the supporting arms were on the road itself. The rate of advance was 100yd per minute.

When 2/43 Battalion reached Makh Khad Ridge, the Axis forces opened up with artillery, continuing to target the Australians until the battalion reached its final objective, Miteiriya Ridge. The tanks of 44 RTR attracted Axis fire; the contribution the British armour made to the assault would be derided, with many an Australian soldier commenting that they sought to be immobilized by a mine to avoid closing with the enemy.

After 2,500yd, B Coy was hit by machine-gun and rifle fire from an Italian position. The position was targeted on the move and the Italians surrendered. A further 1,000yd on, B Coy encountered another position with two MMGs and one anti-tank gun. After B Coy was fired upon 400yd from the Italian position, Captain A.I. Hare, OC B Coy, decided to send 10 Platoon to outflank it while 12 Platoon lay prone and commenced firing. When the flanking move was complete, the Italians appeared with hands held up. The anti-tank gun was the last to stop firing. Some 50 Italian prisoners including an officer were taken. The anti-tank gunner was bayoneted and the gun destroyed.

The artillery bombardment commenced when B Coy was 2,000yd from Miteiriya Ridge and lifted when B Coy was 1,000yd away from the ridge. At 0703hrs, when the company reached the rise by Trig 30, they could see transport vehicles and five tanks immediately ahead, with two tanks and other vehicles on the right. Three enemy tanks and two MMGs to the front opened up. MMGs and mortars targeted the Australians from the right. At 0710hrs, Axis infantry and two tanks could be seen 1,000–1,500yd away forming up for a counter-attack; the Italian attack was soon defeated by small-arms fire from 800yd. Then another four Axis tanks appeared and commenced firing. Hare sent a message to battalion headquarters requesting support as Axis fire was intensifying, but no support was in the offing. At 0730hrs the forward platoon of B Coy was told to withdraw because C Coy was seen to be withdrawing. This instruction was countermanded almost straightaway when D Coy elements could be seen approaching. At 0745hrs the Axis forces attacked in front and battalion headquarters messaged B Coy that a withdrawal was necessary. The forward platoon moved first and took up positions 800yd further back to cover the rest of the company. Four Axis tanks that had taken up hull-down positions on the ridge began firing.

C Coy on the left was not so quick as B Coy; Italian MMGs targeted the left platoon 1,000yd after the assault commenced and had to be neutralized by supporting friendly tanks. The Australians encountered shallow trenches with mines and wire as they passed through the Italian positions. A supporting tank was stopped by an Axis mine. Enemy anti-tank fire destroyed another tank. C Coy thought the Australian artillery forward observer's vehicle probably hit a mine as he was not seen again. Some 800yd further on, C Coy's left platoon had to veer off further left as it met stiff resistance from other Italian positions situated in broken ground. The second-line platoon was brought up to maintain contact with the two forward platoons. Although the right forward platoon had no trouble advancing, the other platoons were delayed getting to the ridge. Only a single man of the left section of the left platoon was not a casualty, Private R.J. Dean. He took up a Bren gun and met up with the other sections of his platoon 1,000yd further on. The platoon commander was killed.

When re-formed on the ridge, C Coy took up defensive positions and then received heavy fire from Axis machine guns, anti-tank guns and field guns. The Australians noticed motor transport departing hastily. Of immediate concern 300yd to the left front of the right forward platoon, three enemy gun-battery positions fired on C Coy. Company headquarters with the left platoon captured these positions by approaching from the flank. A total of 150 prisoners were taken and three guns were destroyed or damaged. The positions held a total of 19 field guns, four anti-tank guns, two MMGs and two LMGs, manned by troops from the I and III/46° Reggimento artiglieria. Captain J.D. Gordon, OC C Coy, decided not to use anti-tank grenades to destroy the other guns as enemy tanks could be seen. C Coy then received the battalion headquarters order to withdraw.

D Coy maintained 500yd distance behind the forward companies. Owing to friendly tanks moving amid the company, enemy shelling was experienced. After 2nd Lieutenant G.D. Combe, OC 18 Platoon, was wounded by shrapnel, Sergeant G. Hartree bandaged him and sent him back with the other wounded on a carrier. Captain Jeanes at the front of the company was wounded and evacuated. When D Coy got to the ridge it continued 500yd forward to protect C Coy's consolidation of the position on the ridge. The men of D Coy could see 500 vehicles and 16 tanks some 1,500yd ahead. The tank commander was asked to bring up his tanks but declined to do so as his strength was depleted, with only six tanks available. D Coy was told to withdraw and did so, herding prisoners and destroying enemy equipment as the Australians returned to Makh Khad Ridge.

By late afternoon, 2/43 Battalion was back on the start line, by the junction. An estimate of 1,000 prisoners taken was reported, with nine anti-tank guns and four field guns, 12 MMGs and three light mortars destroyed. The battalion had two officers and ten other ranks killed, four officers and 62 other ranks wounded (an officer and six other ranks died of wounds later), and three other ranks missing on 17 July. Sergeant W. Curran commanded 18 Platoon and Sergeant-Major H. Hampton commanded 17 Platoon. Lieutenant Grant was temporary company commander. According to 24 Australian Brigade, 29 Italian officers and 707 other ranks were taken prisoner during the 17 July operation.

During the late afternoon, 2/28 Battalion, with two anti-tank troops and a machine-gun platoon under command, was ordered to occupy positions forward of the other two battalions. By 0130hrs on 18 July, a line 1,650yd south-west of the telegraph line along the Qattara Track was occupied without encountering much enemy. Slightly further back, 2/32 and 2/43 battalions occupied a line 1,800yd west of and 1,500yd east of the Qattara Track respectively. At first light on 18 July, 2/28 Battalion observed Axis elements on Point 22.

During the battle, the II/65° Reggimento fanteria motorizzato was surrounded and then overrun. The regimental commander, Colonello Gherardo Vaiarini, was mortally wounded when attempting to break the encirclement. Aufklärungs-Abteilung (mot.) 3 and elements of Kampfgruppe Kiehl had rushed to the area with armoured cars, tanks, anti-tank guns and infantry. Axis counter-attacks pushed back the Australians to their departure line. The rapid deployment of German mobile units, similar in many ways to Ruweisat Ridge, had threatened the destruction of the Australian infantry committed to the assault. This did not happen partly because the Australians had friendly tanks nearby. The New Zealanders had no such support though the Indians did manage to get tank support.

The assessment of Italian strength late on 17 July was grim. 'Brescia' had only a single battalion with no artillery. 'Pavia' had two battalions. 'Ariete' had only a single battalion of *bersaglieri* plus a company's worth of tanks and one gun group. 'Littorio' had similar forces. 'Trieste' had a single artillery group and three battalions. 'Sabratha' had no complete infantry battalions and no guns. Only 'Trento' had experienced no significant losses. During 10–16 July, 'Sabratha' lost 122 officers and 1,846 NCOs and soldiers. Within a week only 1,700 officers and men could be counted on, including 400 from combat-support units.

Late on 17 July, the Axis commanders concluded that Ruweisat Ridge could not be recaptured. Noting that the Allied forces were using their superiority in infantry to destroy the Italian formations, on 18 July Rommel wrote that the previous day's fighting was critical and threatened the collapse of the front (Montanari 2007: 157). Rommel was told that the 'Bologna' Infantry Division was on its way, as well as the 185ª Divisione paracadutisti 'Folgore' and three other infantry divisions. The German 164. leichte Afrika-Division was also en route, plus Fallschirmjäger-Brigade Ramcke and 72 8.8cm guns. Rommel sought to build a fortified system from Qattara to the coast with these units.

An Australian soldier with a captured German MG 34 machine gun, 25 July 1942. Unlike the Vickers gun, the 7.92mm MG 34 fed from the left side of the weapon; it could use drum magazines or belts of ammunition. (piemags/archive/military/Alamy Stock Photo)

Ruweisat Ridge was held on the northern slope forward of Point 64 by the 28° Reggimento di fanteria, the southern slope by the 19° Reggimento di fanteria, and III./PzGrenRgt 104 on Point 63; the German armour took position south of the ridge. On 22 July, 3/7 Rajputs was thrown back by the battalion of 19° Reggimento di fanteria, though Point 63 was temporarily in Allied hands when another Indian battalion took 190 Germans prisoner. Lieutenant-General Gott then sent 23 Armoured Brigade forward despite Major-General A.H. Gatehouse, GOC 10th Armoured Division, protesting the danger of the minefields.

At 0800hrs the British tanks pushed on to El Mrier, south of Ruweisat Ridge. This was the target for the New Zealanders. After losing 30 tanks in the first minefield, 40 RTR and 46 RTR lost further vehicles to mines and when they got to El Mrier a counter-attack by Panzer-Regiment 5 routed them. The Allied infantry had failed; attacking from the south, they had to move north-west, in front of German defences that fired into their flank.

Late on 22 July, 24 Australian Brigade targeted Point 22 on Miteiriya Ridge once again, deploying 2/32 Battalion, A Coy, 2/43 Battalion, and 2/43 Battalion. Two German battalions – I./SR 361 and I./leIR 155 – assisted the 61° Reggimento fanteria motorizzato in protecting the approaches. A Coy, 2/43 Battalion, had 15 killed, including Captain W. Sudholz, the company commander. The tanks of 50 RTR were committed to support 24 Australian Brigade. The III/62° Reggimento fanteria motorizzato and the III/61° Reggimento fanteria motorizzato held the Australian infantry, meaning the British tanks got to the ridge alone; 50 RTR lost 56 tanks. Most British tanks losses could not be recovered from the battlefield as the ground was in Axis hands. Rommel mentioned in dispatches that the III/61° Reggimento fanteria motorizzato had fought brilliantly (Montanari 2007: 215).

Operation *Lightfoot*

24–25 October 1942

BACKGROUND TO BATTLE

By October 1942, Rommel needed to fight a battle of attrition because his fuel shortages inhibited a manoeuvre battle and forced him to station his armour along the whole 40-mile-long front in case of an enemy breakthrough. Rommel assumed that Montgomery would attack with armour first, and that anti-tank mines, in some places laid 6,000yd in depth, would force Montgomery into a lengthy frontal assault to breach them. Rommel's verdict about the importance of armour to Montgomery meant the Axis minefields included only 8 per cent anti-personnel mines. The Axis infantry had to defeat Montgomery's infantry attacks to seize positions to cover combat engineers working to clear lanes through the minefields if Rommel's strategy was to work. A weak Italian outpost line amid the minefields gave Montgomery's infantry an opportunity to establish themselves by the time dawn broke on 24 October. Montgomery would not hurry his offensive, instead ensuring he had trained his forces to a sufficient level for the missions he wanted them to accomplish. Montgomery also knew that the minefields would not permit close tank/infantry cooperation.

While 2nd NZ Division had 9 Armoured Brigade attached, Montgomery did not give an important role to the Indians. His initial plan was to force Miteiriya Ridge with infantry and let armour pass through to occupy the Aqqaqir height situated on the Rahman track, Rommel's supply route to the south. The Deutsches Afrikakorps would be forced to counter-attack. Major-General Lumsden was commanding the armour because Lieutenant-General Horrocks had turned down the appointment. Montgomery then amended the plan to make it a break-in, not a breakthrough. Armour established on Miteiriya Ridge would shield the Allied infantry from enemy armour.

Further infantry assaults would 'crumble' Axis defences, and would force the Deutsches Afrikakorps to counter-attack with armour.

Miteiriya Ridge was the New Zealanders' first objective during the initial stage of the battle, Operation *Lightfoot*. This was the assault by four infantry divisions from XXX Corps through Axis defences built behind a thick belt of minefields. Engineers would follow the infantry to clear gaps in the minefields through which the British tanks of Lumsden's X Corps would advance. The initial Allied attack would be supported by a massive artillery bombardment. Yet only 408 of 1,000 guns supported the main attack. Others would be used on deception bombardments to disguise the main point of effort. Lieutenant-General Freyberg, GOC 2nd NZ Division, then insisted on a creeping artillery barrage to accompany the infantry as they advanced. While 4 Field Artillery Regiment RNZA targeted known enemy defensive positions, 5 and 6 Field Artillery regiments RNZA assisted 5 and 6 NZ brigades with a barrage. The New Zealanders' guns were too few to make this effective, however. Major-General Tuker, GOC 4th Indian Division, insisted the barrage was a wasteful and rigid form of artillery support, holding up successful infantry and deserting the unsuccessful (Wood 2012: 244). Counter-battery fire could not destroy the Axis guns. Neither did it destroy many of the infantry strongpoints. Tuker criticized Montgomery for not concentrating enough guns in the north.

During the action, 2nd NZ Division occupied a 5,000yd section of Miteiriya Ridge: 5 NZ Brigade was to attack on the northern half and 6 NZ Brigade on the southern half of the ridge. At first, each brigade would advance a battalion 3,500yd, which would then stop and entrench. Then the other two battalions of each brigade would advance 3,000yd beyond this to get to the ridge. The battalions would attack on a three-company frontage during both phases. A total of 74 25-pdr field guns and eight 4.5in guns would support the New Zealanders. Elements of 10th Armoured Division would then approach through the gaps in the minefield.

The first phase of 5 NZ Brigade's attack was assigned to 23 NZ Battalion. During the second phase, 21 NZ Battalion was on the right with 22 NZ Battalion on the left. Lieutenant-Colonel R.W. Harding's 21 NZ Battalion

New Zealand troops near Mersa Matruh, June 1942. For many recruits, overseas travel appealed. The men had plenty of leave when deployed. In Egypt during 1940, of 19 NZ Battalion, 20 per cent had evening passes and 66 per cent had weekend passes to go to Cairo. The wage, 35s per week, was good at the time. Pay and rations were better than those of the British soldier. (Mondadori/Getty Images)

had A Coy on the right forward, B Coy in the centre, and C Coy on the left forward. D Coy was behind A Coy, with battalion headquarters to D Coy's left. The forward companies each had two platoons in line forward, five paces between each man with the third platoon in files behind. The company headquarters was in the centre. When the objective was seized D Coy would exploit forward to attack enemy guns with 24 explosive charges. A platoon of MMGs and a troop of 6-pdr anti-tank guns were under command. The operation would commence at 0055hrs on 24 October. A company from 28 Māori Battalion would be behind them to mop up.

At this time, 21 NZ Battalion had four understrength companies each with nine LMGs, totalling 249 men. The companies had an average bayonet strength of 62 men.

The Italians had built infantry strongpoints with barbed wire and extensive minefields to the front. Minefields were covered by field artillery and anti-tank guns. Combat outposts forward of the minefields and some 1,000–2,000yd forward of the main line were occupied. The II/62° Reggimento fanteria motorizzato and the III/61° Reggimento fanteria motorizzato had III. and II./IR 382 of the 164. leichte Afrika-Division between them, to stiffen the defences on Miteiriya Ridge from the Qattara Track to beyond its western end.

Opposing 21 NZ Battalion was the II/62° Reggimento fanteria motorizzato, commanded by Capitano Manassei; II./IR 382 was on its right. Axis minefields were laid out in angled formation in order to force the Allied tanks to turn and expose their weaker side armour to anti-tank guns sited forward. A Coy and B Coy, 21 NZ Battalion, faced the main Italian defences while C Coy on the Italian right had an easier time because this was the

Bersaglieri clear Commonwealth Mk II anti-tank mines, El Alamein, August 1942. Containing about 4lb of TNT, the Mk II was used in large numbers during 1942, being supplanted by the larger Mk V mine by 1945. (Mondadori via Getty Images)

Two New Zealand riflemen, one armed with an SMLE rifle and the other with what appears to be a captured Italian rifle, engage an Axis dive bomber, 20 July 1942. (Daily Mirror/Mirrorpix via Getty Images)

boundary with the Germans. The main barbed wire was in the forward line with a less-dense line forward of the main defences.

The II/62° Reggimento fanteria motorizzato was about 600 strong with 12 47mm anti-tank guns, 12 anti-tank rifles, 12 MMGs and three medium mortars. Most Italian positions lay on the reverse slope of Miteiriya Ridge. This helped protect them though they could not target the attackers effectively. A company was deployed as outposts on the whole battalion front. In addition, the Italian battalion deployed about a company's worth in the 51st (Highland) Division sector. Schneck suggests (2005: 116) that the Italians had 397 men facing the New Zealanders, including the forward company. This company was dispersed, probably with half not opposing 21 NZ Battalion. The defenders had a numerical advantage; Wood states (2012: 247) that 336 men opposed the II/62° Reggimento fanteria motorizzato. The Italians had six MMGs firing on fixed lines, 18 LMGs, six 47mm anti-tank guns, six anti-tank rifles and three mortars in the main battalion position.

The New Zealanders possessed detailed information about the enemy. This was passed down to subunits. Each Italian company had five fire centres (*centri di fuoco*), strongpoints occupied by 16–18 men. Each strongpoint was composed of a main fighting pit in the middle with another pit either side in arrowhead formation, connected by crawl trenches. Four of the strongpoints each had one 47mm anti-tank gun, one Breda 37 MMG and one or two Breda 30 LMGs. The other strongpoint had the same, but with one anti-tank rifle instead of the anti-tank gun. Three strongpoints in the first line were built 200m (219yd) forward of the other two in the second line. Each was 150m (164yd) apart from the next in line.

MAP KEY

1 **0055hrs:** Commencing its advance through 23 NZ Battalion positions, 21 NZ Battalion has A Coy on the right, B Coy in the centre and C Coy on the left, with D Coy 400yd behind A Coy. Preceded by a creeping barrage, the leading New Zealand companies deploy two platoons forward in line with the third in files behind.

2 **0140hrs:** A pause in the creeping barrage sees Major Smith, OC C Coy, send a platoon to establish contact with 22 NZ Battalion on the left.

3 *c.***0200–0240hrs:** D Coy loses formation in the dust and murk behind the forward companies. Corporal McManus assumes command of 17 Platoon and Sergeant Blakely takes charge of 18 Platoon. Lieutenant Robertson, OC 16 Platoon, gathers up those NZ troops he finds.

4 *c.***0240hrs:** Major Smith, OC C Coy, is the only company commander to reach Miteiriya Ridge; C Coy has had the easiest approach. Smith radios Lieutenant-Colonel Harding.

5 *c.***0250–0300hrs:** B Coy reports that it has reached the ridge although Captain Marshall has been killed. By 0300hrs, 21 NZ Battalion signals brigade that the objective has been reached.

6 **0330–0430hrs:** Lieutenant Robertson leads his 16 Platoon and parts of others forward of the ridge to assault Axis gun positions. He is back on the ridge with 90 prisoners by 0430hrs, his platoon having destroyed four 105mm guns, three anti-tank guns and several machine guns.

7 **0630hrs:** A Sqn, Royal Wiltshire Yeomanry, is on the ridge, but does not encounter Axis armour until 25 October.

Battlefield environment

On 24 October, 21 NZ Battalion would assault the western end of Miteiriya Ridge, some 3 miles from the Qattara Track. The Italians had heavily mined Makh Khad and had minor forward positions ahead of the mines. The New Zealanders needed to occupy the western 5,000yd section of Miteiriya Ridge. On the right (west), 5 NZ Brigade would conduct the assault with a single battalion moving 3,500yd and then digging in; the other two battalions of the brigade would then cover a further 3,000yd to the ridge. Each battalion would assault the enemy on a three-company frontage, with each company on a 400yd frontage. During this phase, 21 NZ Battalion was on the right with 22 NZ Battalion on the left. Sufficient moonlight meant the New Zealanders could see each other and locate the objective. They would be concealed adequately from the defenders who

had a line of sight during daylight. The minefields would cause casualties, but would not hold the New Zealanders up much. The lack of natural obstacles aided control.

The Italians had the II/62° Reggimento fanteria motorizzato defending the western end of the ridge, with II./IR 382 to its right. The main Italian defence zone was behind the ridge, thereby denying them the ability to target the assaulting infantry on the other side of the ridge. Only one company occupied positions forward of the ridge. The dispersed nature of Italian strongpoints, constructed to minimize the effect of bombardments, meant they could not support each other during the hours of darkness. Smoke and dust further reduced visibility, permitting the New Zealanders to close with the isolated defenders' weapon pits.

Italian troops under aerial bombardment, El Alamein, 26 October 1942. (Keystone/Getty Images)

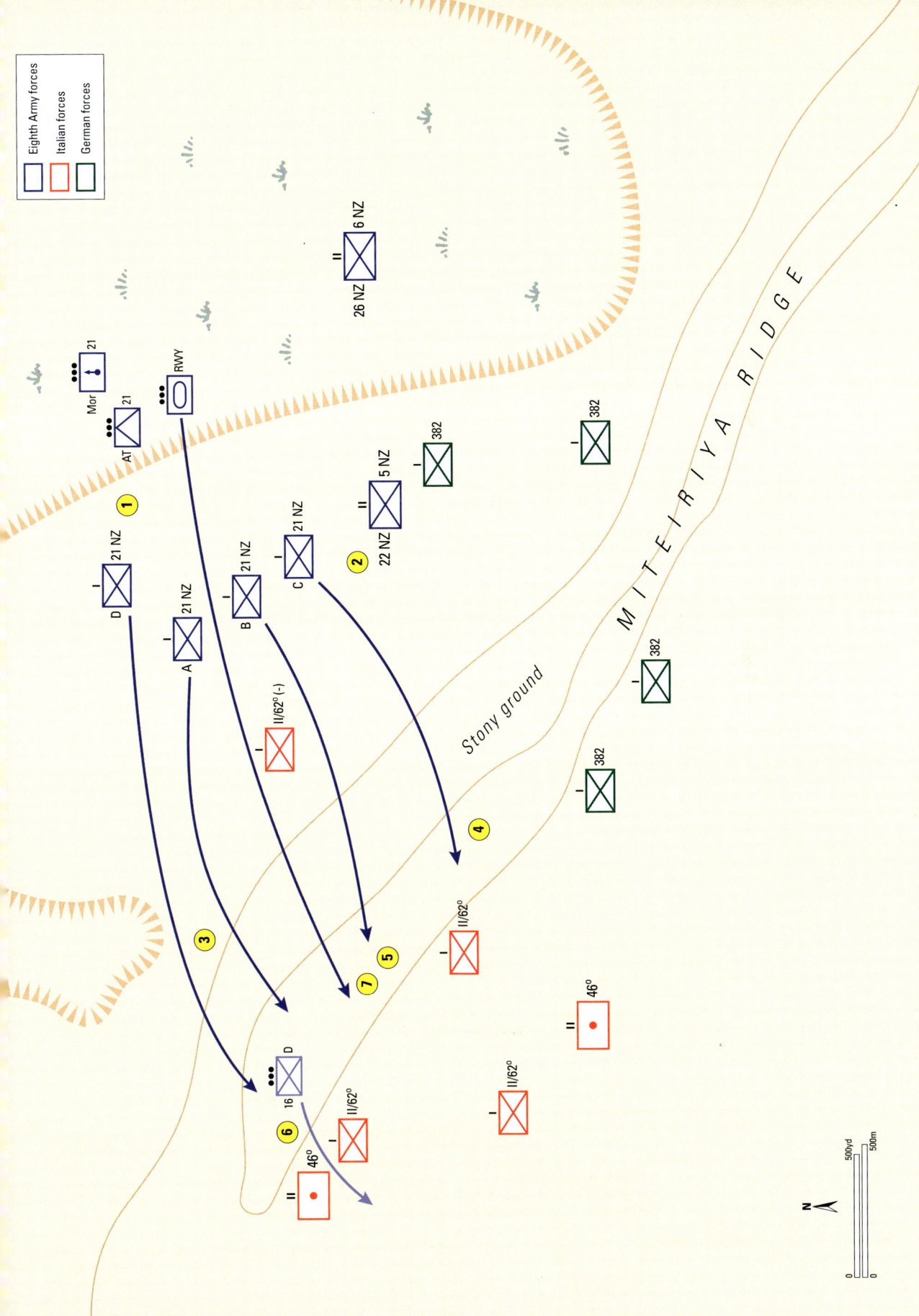

Eighth Army forces

Italian forces

German forces

6 NZ

26 NZ

21 Mor

21

RWY

21 AT

382

5 NZ

382

22 NZ

1

21 NZ
D

21 NZ
A

21 NZ
B

21 NZ
C

2

382

II/62° (-)

Stony ground

382

MITEIRIYA RIDGE

4

II/62°

3

5

7

46°

16 D

II/62°

6

II/62°

46°

N

500yd
500m

INTO COMBAT

At 2140hrs on 23 October the Allied artillery bombardment, conducted by 480 guns, commenced. Enemy guns were targeted for 15 minutes, then the Axis forward positions for about half an hour. The creeping artillery barrage began soon afterwards. Under bright moonlight, 21 NZ Battalion advanced on the Italian positions at 0055hrs on 24 October. Miteiriya Ridge only had a 30ft ascent. The battalion had to advance 4,000yd to get to the first Axis positions. The battalion frontage was 1,200yd, the company frontage was 400yd with another behind. The moonlight permitted leaders to navigate and coordinate the approach. The dark gave them cover. The defenders had little cover forward of the ridge and therefore decided to deploy most forces on the reverse slope; but this denied them visibility of the attackers.

The barrage was supposed to linger for three minutes and then be moved further forward by 100yd. The Allied infantry could not in many cases keep up with the barrage. The barrage also highlighted the extent of the advance to the Axis forces and could not halt to wait for Allied infantry to catch up or stop if the infantry was outpacing the barrage. The bombardment had not destroyed many Axis positions. Each Allied gun had a frontage of 46yd. The bombardment was not prolonged. Instead the New Zealanders needed to attack Italian strongpoints in close combat.

Minefields caused Allied casualties though not delays. Also mortars and guns opened up on the New Zealanders, causing additional losses. Many explosions were caused by the detonation of anti-personnel mines. Coordination between Allied subunits was helped by radio contact between Lieutenant-Colonel Harding and his company commanders.

When Italian positions were encountered this often happened at close range. A platoon engaged a position frontally while a section enveloped around the flank to close with the bayonet. The supporting sections suppressed the

Bersaglieri with a 20mm Solothurn anti-tank rifle. Heavy, long and difficult to use owing to its substantial recoil, this Swiss weapon was adopted by the Italians in 1940, and was mainly used on vehicle mounts. (SeM/ Universal Images Group via Getty Images)

Italians and distracted them to assist the final close-quarter battle fought by the flanking soldiers. This was the method Sergeant H.J. Bramwell used; he deployed two sections to engage the enemy and took a third around the flank to assault the position. With only a section closing with the enemy, communication and control was relatively straightforward.

At 0055hrs, the first smoke shells landed to signal the time 21 NZ Battalion would commence its assault. Strung-out New Zealand platoons advanced through the drifting smoke. Tracer fired from Italian positions on fixed lines could be seen cutting through the fog. When contact was lost temporarily with 22 NZ Battalion on the right, Major N.B. Smith, OC C Coy, sent his second-line platoon to re-establish contact.

Harding used his radio to maintain communication with his companies. He did not need to make many decisions during the attack because it was heavily scripted. His situational awareness was good, and he heard of the loss of Captain W.C. Butland, OC A Coy, on the ridge. Harding told Lieutenant K.C. West-Watson, a platoon commander in D Coy, to take charge of A Coy; West-Watson was himself wounded shortly afterwards. Prior to the battle

A New Zealand Vickers gun team, El Alamein, July 1942. A water-cooled weapon, the venerable .303 Vickers was renowned for its reliability. (Trinity Mirror/Mirrorpix/ Alamy Stock Photo)

commencing, Brigadier Kippenberger had told Harding that the right-hand company would have the hardest task (Kippenberger 1949: 226). Harding did not want a platoon commander worrying about the company and his own platoon at the same time. Lieutenant B.S. Catran, a platoon commander of A Coy, was also killed and his platoon was led by Sergeant C.D.M. Klaus.

B Coy also had a hard time, with Captain J.R.B. Marshall, OC B Coy, being killed. Junior officers and NCOs assumed command because officer casualties were high, partly because they had to move between platoons and sections to maintain situational awareness. Lieutenant A.T. Eady took command of B Coy.

The only company commander to reach the final objective was Major Smith, OC C Coy. His company's approach having been relatively straightforward, Smith reported to Harding by radio that C Coy was on the ridge. The success signal was sent by 21 NZ Battalion to 5 NZ Brigade at 0300hrs on 24 October, at which time the NZ companies dug in on the ridge. Cable was then laid to get a telephone network up and running.

On the right, Captain B.M. Laird's D Coy had a hard time, having lost contact in the dust thrown up by battle. Sergeant E.H. Blakey had to take charge of 18 Platoon after 2nd Lieutenant J.P. Stranger was wounded. The officer commanding 17 Platoon along with the platoon sergeant were soon casualties. Corporal T. McManus found he had to take command; by the time the platoon reached the objective only five men remained. He then gathered men from 16 and 18 platoons he found and then Lieutenant P. Robertson appeared with part of 16 Platoon. Despite these losses, D Coy, down to a single platoon in strength by the time it reached the ridge, could exploit further and with Robertson commanding, destroyed four 105mm

An Italian gun crew, 25 October 1942. This is a Breda 20/65 mod. 35 anti-aircraft gun utilized in the ground role. By October 1942, 'Trento' had two eight-gun batteries, as part of its artillery regiment. (Keystone-France/Gamma-Keystone via Getty Images)

Bersaglieri during October 1942. Note the middle soldier with a Breda 30 LMG; fed by 20-round stripper clips, it was considered to be an unreliable weapon, prone to jamming and overheating. The magazine, located on the right side of the weapon, could not be detached and had to be loaded with rounds from a stripper clip. If the magazine was damaged the weapon was useless until repaired by the unit armourer. The method by which cartridge cases were extracted was too rapid during the primary phase, meaning they often got stuck. To remedy this, each round was lubricated prior to entering the chamber. In the desert, sand attached itself to the oiled rounds and caused even worse problems. Also, because rounds were fired from a closed bolt, the weapon could not be cooled by air circulating through an open bolt. This sometimes led to rounds firing off without the gunner knowing. (Roger Violet via Getty Images)

guns, three anti-tank guns and several MMGs. He took 90 prisoners. Patrols had to be in by 0430hrs and Robertson got back to the ridge by then. First light was 0630hrs.

The cost of the initial attack was a staggering 122 NZ casualties: 37 killed, including four officers; 83 wounded, including five officers; and two missing. Nine of 16 officers of 21 NZ Battalion ended up as casualties during the attack. The battalion took 130 prisoners. A squadron from the Royal Wiltshire Yeomanry (9 Armoured Brigade) was with 21 NZ Battalion by dawn, but lost some tanks in the minefields.

With 6 NZ Brigade not having kept pace, 5 NZ Brigade was out in front and on the forward slope exposed to machine-gun and mortar fire. No Axis

New Zealand troops man slit trenches, El Alamein, 3 August 1942. The 2NZEF's rank and file displayed a certain belligerent scepticism towards officers. Deference and formality were not part of New Zealand society as they were in Britain. Officers had to know when to tolerate infringements and when not to let discipline slide. (Associated Press/Alamy Stock Photo)

Miteiriya Ridge, 24 October 1942 (previous pages)

This scene depicts an MMG weapons pit on the reverse slope of Miteiriya Ridge during the early-morning hours. The Breda 37 was the standard Italian MMG; here, the weapon is mounted on a plinth of rock and is firing at soldiers of 21 NZ Battalion on the crest of the ridge. The Breda 37 used 20-round ammunition trays; some trays full of empty cartridges can be seen on the ground and plinth. The loader is reaching for the ammunition box for extra trays. An LMG gunner with a Breda 30 LMG is on the right, by a crawl trench. He suspects the New Zealanders to have infiltrated into the adjacent weapons pit. The officer, a *sottotenente*, has the insignia of the 62° Reggimento fanteria motorizzato on his shoulder boards.

counter-attack materialized during the day, which was just as well because friendly tanks had moved south to assist 6 NZ Brigade. By the morning of 25 October, the supporting arms, including MMGs, anti-tank guns and tanks, were in position with 21 NZ Battalion. The British tanks could not maintain position on Miteiriya Ridge during the day, at best taking up hull-down positions behind the ridge. Artillery observers on the ridge brought in battery fire against Axis tanks at long range and stalled the enemy counter-attack in its tracks. On 26 October the enemy tried again with tanks during late afternoon with the same consequences. After dark, 21 NZ Battalion was withdrawn; D Coy was disbanded. Altogether, 21 NZ Battalion had suffered 128 casualties. The battalion had a break until 4 November when with Operation *Supercharge* complete, 2nd NZ Division was ordered to accompany 4 Light Armoured Brigade to Fuka, 50 miles to the west. By the morning of 5 November, the headquarters of the 'Trento' Motorized Division were taken prisoner south of Fuka escarpment.

German counter-attacks did not work effectively. After returning from leave on 25 October, Rommel stopped the armour counter-attacks. The Australians continued 'crumbling' operations further north, forcing Rommel to commit the 90. leichte Afrika-Division, his reserve. When this was achieved, Montgomery switched from 'crumbling' operations to seeking a breakthrough.

An Italian 75/27 modello 06 gun with its crew. Designed by Krupp in 1906, this weapon was assigned to artillery regiments; it could fire HEAT rounds, though only out to 765yd. The Italian gunners were considered to be particularly effective. (SeM/ Universal Images Group via Getty Images)

Analysis

Rommel praised the Italian soldiers as disciplined, sober, and excellent workers (Montanari 2007: 175). They could build good entrenchments. He thought they lacked training, though, and could not attack properly. Many operations failed because of a lack of coordination with the artillery. Shortages of motor transport meant the Italians could not form up as whole units and they could not be utilized as higher-formation reserves because they could not respond quickly.

Rommel was so successful up to July 1942 because British commanders had no proper combined-arms doctrine upon which they could agree. Allied commanders argued with each other and senior officers failed to manage disputes. The desert terrain exposed the infantry to armour because entrenching was difficult and they had little opportunity to conceal positions. Operation *Crusader* had seen British armoured divisions' support groups (artillery and infantry) fighting independently from armour. They formed 'Jock' columns to raid Axis lines of communication. Only XIII Corps and the Tobruk garrison had pursued successful assaults with tanks and infantry combining closely. Training manuals mandated this approach though not many commanders used them.

Instead, Major-General Corbett advocated dispersion of armour to confuse the enemy, mobility to surprise him and the separation of armour from infantry so the tanks did not get slowed down by the infantry. This, Corbett thought, would counter massed German tank assaults. He wanted brigade groups and not divisional groupings to be the basis of unit organization and taught area defence. A fortress system of infantry strongpoints would be used as pivots by the armour. Tuker, a colonel and Corbett's deputy in 1940, thought the armoured divisions' support groups should be abolished, though he did believe the armoured division should fight alongside the infantry division. During Operation *Crusader*, Major-General Freyberg insisted his New Zealanders had 4 Armoured Brigade detached from 7th Armoured Division to guard against

Axis armour, even though Freyberg already had a brigade of infantry-support tanks assigned to him. Although the Allied infantry was better protected, this approach exposed British armour to defeat in detail. Composed of Royal Tank Regiment (RTR) units, 4 Armoured Brigade gained the best results during Operation *Crusader* because the armour cooperated with infantry. Composed of Territorial Army yeomanry units, 22 Armoured Brigade had little training with infantry. Deploying by January 1942, 2 Armoured Brigade operated with its support group detached and was defeated piecemeal.

Only infantry cooperating with tanks wore down the Axis forces during Operation *Crusader*, leading to the relief of Tobruk. Tank battalions needed to train with the infantry with whom they would cooperate in battle, or so thought RTR officers. Norrie and Gott, however, continued to maintain brigade boxes and 'Jock' columns were utilized. Major General A.F. Harding, Deputy Director of Military Training Middle East Command during January–September 1942, taught infantry to build brigade boxes using 25-pdr field guns to keep Axis tanks at bay. From March 1942, the British established a defence line of mines running 50 miles south of Gazala and 30 miles west of Tobruk so the port was out of range of German guns, defended by brigade boxes with armour roving about outside them. Boxes further back also guarded supply dumps at Belhamed. Armour was tied to the defence of these boxes. Motor brigades also formed boxes, limiting their mobility.

Italian troops on the march alongside a heavily laden truck. In theory, the divisional transport included 398 lorries and 34 tractors to haul the guns, but even on paper the Italian infantry division did not possess sufficient transport and supply units to make the formation self-sufficient. Army-level supply units were responsible for supplying units. This centralization kept division size low and was supposed to make them agile and quick, though it needed an efficient organization to achieve this. Forward units found this reliance on higher-formation army units hampered rather than supported them. (ullstein bild/ ullstein bild via Getty Images)

During the fighting at Gazala, Rommel was assisted by the failure of British armour to support the infantry. By May 1942, British armoured commanders exhibited a substantial amount of caution, partly because of the effectiveness of German 8.8cm guns. On 30 May 1942, Major-General Lumsden failed to assault the positions of the 'Ariete' Armoured Division when Rommel with his armour was stuck behind British boxes in the Cauldron, wanting the Axis gun line to be dealt with by an infantry assault first. The opportunity to hit Rommel's German armour, tied up assaulting 150 Brigade box, was lost as Lumsden's plan needed time to organize and in the end was cancelled because of a sandstorm. Rommel demolished the box on 1 June. The British planned another attempt to destroy Rommel in the Cauldron before the remaining boxes were overrun. Although the South Africans refused to participate, Major-General Sir H.R. Briggs, GOC 5th Indian Division, did take part, though he thought the attack was to be an envelopment. Major-General F.W. Messervy, GOC 7th Armoured Division, changed the plan to a frontal assault. The subsequent operation would influence the way infantry commanders thought of armour.

The plan was for infantry battalions belonging to 9 and 10 Indian brigades to break enemy defences on 5 June and form boxes within the Axis position; 22 Armoured Brigade and an infantry tank brigade would assist. The Indian brigades had never previously operated with tanks. No commander-in-chief with authority over 5th Indian and 7th Armoured divisions was appointed to command the operation. An unidentified 9 Indian Brigade company commander explained that the tank squadron assigned to his battalion

These seven Australian officers are about to be presented with gallantry decorations by Lieutenant-General Sir Leslie J. Morshead, 9 September 1942. Note the variety of ways in which the side-arms are carried, and the nearest man's use of the revolver lanyard. (Associated Press/Alamy Stock Photo)

soon departed without contacting the battalion commander (Colvin 2020: 162). His battalion was severely handled by Axis tanks. The British tank commanders thought exploitation and not assault was the role they needed to adopt. The infantry, though, only had 2-pdrs to protect them. Halted by Italian artillery fire, 22 Armoured Brigade reported that most of its 60 tank losses were caused by mechanical breakdowns. Then a German tank assault destroyed 10 Indian Brigade. Brigadier B.C. Fletcher, OC 9 Indian Brigade, was critical, stating that no attempt was made to assist him (Colvin 2020: 163). Infantry boxes, Fletcher said, could not be established quickly and needed 48 hours to build. He was subsequently sacked. On 12 June Rommel was free to mass his armour; he isolated Tobruk and Eighth Army withdrew to the frontier.

This lack of cooperation between Allied infantry and British tank commanders plagued the July 1942 operations and had disappointing consequences for the Ruweisat Ridge operation. Lumsden changed the emphasis of orders from Eighth Army, telling the armour to be prepared to deploy to support the infantry and not, as he told Briggs in front of Kippenberger, ordering them to be on the ridge by dawn. If each infantry brigade had a supporting tank regiment deployed with it when the operation commenced then the whole of the ridge could have been held against Axis counter-attacks, not just the Indian portion. It was essential for the tank and infantry units being deployed together to train together prior to the assault. Even though the Australian infantry had Crusaders of 9th Divisional Cavalry supporting them, they found coordination difficult.

By October 1942, the importance of getting armour to support infantry quickly after the initial attack was fully recognized. The same counter-attacks by Axis armour on penetrations made by the infantry as happened in July would not be seen on Miteiriya Ridge, however. Instead, with the ridge lost, the Italians occupied infantry positions further back that had been established when the line was static. The artillery support available to the New Zealanders also made any such Axis counter-attack with armour dangerous. At Ruweisat Ridge, the guns supported the New Zealanders by targeting Axis strongpoints bypassed by the initial assault. The Allied gunners could not target beyond the ridge because of range issues and the inability to correct the fire with no observers on the ridge. At Miteiriya Ridge, the Allied forces gave sufficient attention to dealing with the Italian positions lying on the approaches to the ridge, and the guns could be moved up. Also, the Axis defenders had not made the forward slope a priority; at Ruweisat Ridge, the many Italian positions on the forward slope hampered the consolidation of Indian control on the ridge.

By October, Rommel assumed that Montgomery would attack with armour first. Anti-tank minefields, in some places 6,000yd in depth, would force Montgomery into a lengthy frontal assault to breach them. Rommel needed to fight a battle of attrition because his lack of fuel inhibited a manoeuvre battle. The minefields had only 8 per cent anti-personnel mines, however, so infantry attacks to seize positions to cover engineers working to clear lanes through them needed to be defeated by Rommel's infantry if the Axis strategy was to work. A weak Axis outpost line amid the minefields gave attacking Allied infantry an opportunity to establish positions on Ruweisat Ridge by the time dawn broke.

The training Montgomery demanded prior to the start of Operation *Lightfoot* made 21 NZ Battalion aware of the difficulties the New Zealanders would encounter assaulting Miteiriya Ridge in the dark. Supporting artillery barrages with live rounds were used during these practices, which took place during the dark hours in moonlight, with tracer fired at them on brigade boundaries. Kippenberger thought the exercises were invaluable and gave some experience to be going on with (Kippenberger 1949: 222). Any procedural or organizational weaknesses could be identified and corrected. A broad front was used to make sure as many Axis positions as possible were neutralized and not left alone to interfere with Allied mine-clearance operations and the bringing to the front of support weapons during daylight.

After Ruweisat Ridge, 21 NZ Battalion maintained good morale because plenty of free time was incorporated into the training schedule. The men knew artillery, tanks and aircraft would support them this time. Morale was high despite the apprehensiveness soldiers experienced prior to the attack. In combat they accepted casualties and called out the dangers as they had done during the rehearsals. This, when combined with the group cohesion possessed by men who had gone through the summer battles together, got them through. Tactical problems experienced because of unexpected events, such as the loss of an officer or NCO, could be solved.

Montgomery then continued the infantry battle because his armour could not maintain position on Miteiriya Ridge during the day. Bunching up around lanes made through the minefields further made the British tanks good targets. The infantry battle persisted, with Montgomery throwing forward infantry battalions through the penetrations supported by 6-pdr anti-tank guns, provoking the Axis forces to counter-attack. When they did so, German and Italian tank strength was depleted. Rommel was forced to commit his last reserve, the 90. leichte Afrika-Division, when the Australians struck near the coast. Montgomery then knew a last set-piece assault conducted by infantry to break the enemy line, Operation *Supercharge*, would lead to a breakthrough after the final Axis gun line was broken by 9 Armoured Brigade. By this point, Rommel's tank forces could not counter the British armour.

Italian prisoners of war under Allied guard enter a barbed-wire enclosure, El Alamein, November 1942. (British Official Photo/Wikimedia/Public Domain)

Aftermath

In early February 1943, 3/10 Baluch left 5 Indian Brigade for Cairo. The battalion trained to be a beach unit to assist with Operation *Husky*, the Allied invasion of Sicily during July 1943, operating as separate companies. On 26 August the battalion was together again for Operation *Slapstick*, the landing of British forces at the port of Taranto on the Italian mainland on 9 September. Little combat was seen, and the battalion was sent to Bari, only joining 7 Indian Brigade for combat operations in the Orsagna sector during April 1944. On 14 June the battalion rejoined 5 Indian Brigade and trained for warfare in the Apennines with 4th Indian Division. During August the battalion was the first unit to breach the Gothic Line in northern Italy. By October the brigade was out of the line and was sent to Greece. The battalion returned to India in January 1946.

A young Indian soldier on leave in Cairo, 12 November 1942. (Associated Press/ Alamy Stock Photo)

During March 1943, 2nd NZ Division helped Eighth Army break through the Mareth Line in southern Tunisia. The division then had 4 NZ Infantry Brigade made into 4 NZ Armoured Brigade. By November they had deployed to Italy, fighting on the Sangro River and for Orsagna during December with 21 NZ Battalion part of 5 NZ Brigade. Along with 4th Indian Division they assaulted Monte Cassino during March 1944. They then worked with 8th and 10th Indian divisions pursuing the enemy after Rome was taken. The division found its use of armour restricted by the mountainous terrain and the infantry brigades got an extra infantry battalion to cope. In the event, 21 NZ Battalion stayed until October 1945, occupying Trieste.

Part of the important infantry attack Montgomery needed to persuade Rommel to commit his last reserves prior to Operation *Supercharge*, 2/43 Battalion suffered losses of 108 men on 1 November, including 43 killed, defending the location known as the 'Blockhouse' on the railway. During January 1943, 9th Australian Division departed for the Pacific. On 1 March the convoy reached Adelaide, South Australia, where the battalion disembarked for leave. On 6 April the battalion arrived in Queensland and spent four months training in jungle warfare; 338 replacements were required.

Of the Italian formations, the 'Pavia' Infantry Division was deployed at the southern end of the Axis line during October 1942 and fought next to the 'Folgore' Airborne Division. They held most positions because the assault was mostly designed to be diversionary. When the front broke up, most of the Italians could not keep pace with the Axis withdrawal because they had to move on foot. Some made it to Mersa Matruh, where most surrendered on 7 November. 'Pavia' was officially disbanded on 25 November.

By 25 October, the 'Trento' Motorized Division had lost half its strength defending Miteiriya Ridge. During Operation *Supercharge* they would mostly disappear, fighting alongside the 'Ariete' Armoured Division. Although the division was disbanded on 25 November, some would fight on with 'Trieste'.

During the initial stages of Operation *Lightfoot* the 'Trieste' Motorized Division, the Axis reserve, deployed in the north on 26 October. On 2 November the British hit the division's positions, isolating the battalions of the 65° Reggimento fanteria motorizzato. On 4 November, the 66° Reggimento fanteria motorizzato managed to get back to Fuka; by 26 November at El Agheila this formation was organized in two battalions, each with two companies, with another battalion composed of men not from 'Trieste'. By February 1943, the 'Trieste' companies formed a single battalion. The 65° Reggimento fanteria motorizzato had a battalion composed of its own survivors plus men from 'Pavia' and the 'Brescia' Infantry Division; men from the 'Bologna' Infantry Division composed another battalion and personnel from 'Trento' a third. In this iteration, 'Trieste' would go on to fight on the Mareth Line.

ABOVE LEFT
Pictured in Sydney, these Australian soldiers have just returned from Egypt. (Fairfax Media via Getty Images)

ABOVE RIGHT
Bersaglieri in retreat, El Alamein, November 1942. Bersaglieri adopted the defence-minded 1942 reorganization, but this did not suite the mobile offensive role they were supposed to perform. Despite this, their stubborn defence of positions at El Alamein prompted Rommel to praise them. During the El Alamein fighting, three of four Bersaglieri regiments were destroyed. (Mondadori via Getty Images)

UNIT ORGANIZATIONS

Commonwealth infantry battalion

The Commonwealth infantry battalion included an HQ Coy and four rifle companies. HQ Coy had signals, air-defence, mortar, carrier, administrative (transport) and anti-tank platoons. By 1942, the mortar platoon had six 3in mortars, with a range of 2,800yd. Each mortar was transported dismantled by a carrier, also carrying 66 bombs. Each rifle company was commonly issued with a single mortar from the mortar platoon, with the others forming a reserve.

The rifle company's three rifle platoons each had three sections and a 2in mortar team, with a single anti-tank rifle attached to platoon headquarters. By April 1942, the mortar team and anti-tank rifle were deleted; company headquarters was issued with two 2in mortars. MMGs were operated by machine-gun battalions, with each infantry division possessing such assets. By June 1942, Middle East establishment machine-gun battalions had four companies, each with eight MMGs and four 2-pdr anti-tank guns. The headquarters element of each company also had a 3in mortar.

By April 1942 each Commonwealth infantry battalion in the Middle East was authorized to possess eight 2-pdr anti-tank guns, each of which was carried 'portee' on a 3-ton flat-bed lorry. This means of transportation aided mobility, but it was also advantageous to enemy gunners as it presented them with a bigger target.

Italian infantry regiment

By the end of 1941, the official North Africa-type *reggimento di motorizzata* organization was two *battaglioni fucilieri*, plus a *battaglione armi d'accompagnemento e controcarro* with an 81mm mortar company, an anti-tank company with 47/32 guns and a 20mm gun company. An infantry battalion had three infantry companies plus a weapons company (*compagnia armi d'accompagnmento*).

Each *compagnia fanteria* (infantry company) of this type had three *plotoni fucilieri* (rifle platoons), a *plotone mitragliatrici* (MMG platoon) with two sections each with two Breda 37 MMGs and a command platoon. The *plotone fucilieri* (rifle platoon) had two rifle squads (*squadre fucilieri*) each of 20 men with two Breda 30 LMGs, divided into a rifle group (*gruppo fucile*) and machine-gun group (*gruppo fucili mitragliatori*).

The battalion's weapon company had an MMG platoon operating with a platoon of four 47/32 anti-tank guns.

By mid-1942 the infantry units of the motorized and semi-motorized units had the same organization, with the weapons company assets decentralized to the four infantry companies. The infantry regiment had three rifle battalions and an 81mm mortar company. Each battalion had four companies, each with a command squad, a rifle platoon of 35 men with three squads (each squad with two LMGs), an MMG platoon with 32 men operating three MMGs, an anti-tank platoon with three 20mm or 25mm guns, and an anti-tank platoon with three 47/32 guns.

SELECT BIBLIOGRAPHY

Colvin, J. (2020). *Eighth Army Versus Rommel: Tactics, Training and Operations*. Solihull: Helion & Co.

Greco, F. (2016). *I Leoni di Takrouna: Il 66o Reggimento fanteria Trieste in Africa settentrionale (1941–1943)*. Milan: Biblion Edizioni.

Johnston, M. (2018). *An Australian Band of Brothers: Don Company, Second 43rd Battalion, 9th Division*. Sydney: NewSouth Publishing.

Kippenberger, Maj-Gen Sir H. (1949). *Infantry Brigadier*. Oxford: Oxford University Press. Available at https://nzetc.victoria.ac.nz/tm/scholarly/tei-KipInfa.html (accessed 17 April 2024).

Loi, S. (1983). *Aggredisci e vincerai: Storia della divisione motorizzata 'Trieste'*. Milan: Mursia.

Maxwell, Lt-Col W. (2009). *Capital Campaigners: The History of the 3rd Battalion, The Baluch Regiment*. Uckfield: Naval & Military Press.

Montanari, M. (2007). *The Three Battles of El Alamein, June–November 1942*. Rome: Ufficio Storico dello Stato Maggiore dell'Esercito.

Riccio, R. & Afiero, M. (2021). *Luck was Lacking, but Valour was Not: The Italian Army in North Africa, 1940–43*. Solihull: Helion & Co.

Schneck, W. (2005). *Breaching the Devil's Garden: The 6th New Zealand Brigade in Operation Lightfoot, the Second Battle of El Alamein*. Fort Belvoir, VA: Countermine Division. Available at https://apps.dtic.mil/sti/pdfs/ADA447540.pdf (accessed 17 April 2024).

Sullivan, B.R. (1997). 'The Italian Combat Soldier in Combat 1940–September 1943', in P. Addison & A. Calder, eds, *Time to Kill: The Soldier's Experience in the West, 1939–1945*. London: Pimlico: pp. 177–205.

Wood, P. (2012). 'A Battle to Win: An Analysis of Combat Effectiveness through the Second World War Experience of the 21st (Auckland) Battalion.' Unpublished thesis, Massey University. Available at https://mro.massey.ac.nz/server/api/core/bitstreams/c626d40c-29d9-4e61-821e-184397db786e/content (accessed 17 April 2024).

War Diaries of 2nd AIF (AWM52). Available at https://www.awm.gov.au/collection/C1359733 (accessed 17 April 2024).

Pictured in December 1941, a kneeling squad commander directs his prone Breda 30 gunners. Each Italian rifle squad had two Breda 30 LMGs; this allocation might seem generous, but the peculiarities of these weapons meant they had the characteristics of automatic rifles and not light machine guns. (Keystone-France/Gamma-Keystone via Getty Images)

INDEX

References to illustrations are shown in **bold**. References to plates are shown in bold with caption pages in brackets, e.g. **40–41**, (42).